English for NSW YEAR 7

– STAGE 4 –

Emily Beach

First published in 2023

Insight Publications Pty Ltd
3/350 Charman Road
Cheltenham Victoria 3192
Australia

Tel: +61 3 8571 4950
Fax: +61 3 8571 0257
Email: books@insightpublications.com.au

www.insightpublications.com.au

A catalogue record for this book is available from the National Library of Australia

English for NSW, Year 7, Stage 4 / Emily Beach

ISBN:

9781923016248

Edited by Hannah Cartmel
Proofread by Fiona Wallace
Cover by Melisa Paredes
Internal design by Federico Fonseca and Sardine
Printed by Markono Print Media Pte Ltd

CONTENTS

Unit 1: I've got something to say 2

Chapter 1: Texts that reflect us 5

Chapter 2: Texts that persuade 17

Chapter 3: Texts that share my voice 32

Unit 1: Summative assessment 45

Unit 2: Word of mouth 48

Chapter 4: The traditions of storytelling 51

Chapter 5: Giving words a voice 63

Chapter 6: Words on stage 79

Unit 2: Summative assessment 94

CONTENTS

Unit 3: Of beauty, rich and rare 96

Chapter 7: The land down under 99

Chapter 8: The depths of the ocean 115

Chapter 9: The endless sky 131

Unit 3: Summative assessment 147

Unit 4: Kids these days 150

Chapter 10: Teens in texts 153

Chapter 11: The hunt for the modern teen 165

Chapter 12: Challenging stereotypes to celebrate youth 181

Unit 4: Summative assessment 192

Acknowledgements *194*

Notes *195*

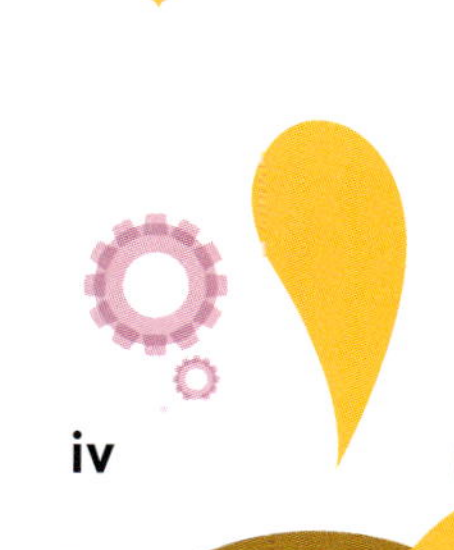

UNIT 01

I've got something to say

Unit inquiry question:
How can texts share who we are and what is most important to us?

In this unit, students will explore how texts can reflect personal experiences, contexts and identity. They will also discover how texts can be a vehicle to express personal opinions and have different voices in the world. Students will engage with a range of nonfiction and fiction texts that express perspectives relative to different contexts and circumstances.

To address the focus inquiry question of the unit, students will engage with learning in three chapters:

Chapter 1
Texts that reflect us

In this chapter, students will explore how texts such as autobiographies and memoirs reflect personal context and perspectives. Students will be invited to make personal connections between their own context and the texts they study.

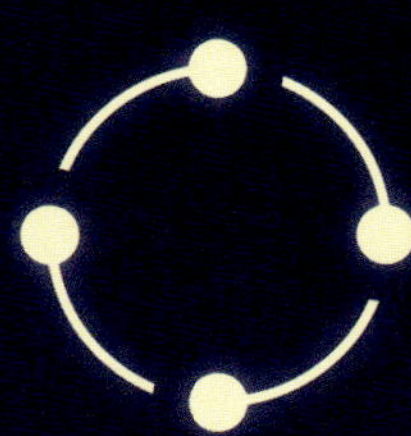

Chapter 2
Texts that persuade

In this chapter, students will explore the features of persuasive texts. They will compare persuasive texts that share similar forms, features, structures and themes. Students will be encouraged to draw connections to their own reading experiences and compare the representation of perspectives concerning issues of importance in our world.

Chapter 3
Texts that share my voice

In this final chapter, students will develop and refine their own perspective on what is most important in our contemporary world and use their reading experiences to compose a personal, persuasive text that shares their perspective on an issue of importance.

The learning activities within each chapter and the summative assessment options (on page 45) provide opportunities to assess student achievement of the following outcomes:

Outcome and Focus Area	Content point
EN4-RVL-01	**Reading, viewing and listening skills**
Reading, viewing and listening to texts	Apply reading pathways to determine form, purpose and meaning Revisit texts to develop a clear understanding of the themes, ideas and attitudes they express
EN4-URB-01	**Perspective and context**
Understanding and responding to texts B	Understand how all perspectives are shaped by language and text Examine how elements of personal and social contexts can inform the perspective and purpose of texts and influence creative decisions
	Argument
	Analyse how engaging personal voice is constructed in texts through linguistic and stylistic choices, and experiment with these choices in own texts
EN4-ECA-01	**Representing**
Expressing ideas and composing texts A	Apply codes and conventions of written, spoken, visual and multimodal texts to enhance meaning and create tone, atmosphere and mood
	Text features: persuasive
	Compose persuasive texts that present arguments from a range of viewpoints, including their own, and that reflect a broadening understanding of perspectives beyond immediate experience
EN4-ECB-01	**Planning, monitoring and revising**
Expressing ideas and composing texts B	Engage with the features and structures of model texts to plan and consider implications for own text creation

CHAPTER 1

TEXTS THAT REFLECT US

Chapter overview

In this chapter you will explore how texts can reflect who we are, our personal context and our perspectives.

You will read about other people's contexts and the factors that have influenced their identity and perspectives. You will also compose your own text that shares a personal experience, inspired by your reading in this chapter.

Success criteria: In this chapter, I will be successful when I can ...

- identify the influences that shape our personal context
- identify features of texts that share personal experiences
- recognise how personal context contributes to the message of a text
- discuss how texts can share perspectives on important issues
- compose a text that reflects a personal experience, inspired by my reading in this chapter.

Chapter inquiry questions

- What influences our personal context?
- What is a perspective and how do texts share them?
- How can I share a personal experience in a text of my own, inspired by my reading experiences?

Key vocabulary

- Context
- Perspective
- Autobiography
- Memoir
- Voice

What influences our personal context?

We all have different personal circumstances: for example, our family structure, ethnic background, education, hobbies and interests. These are all part of our **personal context.** These factors contribute to the unique beliefs, values and perspectives that make up our identity. Our **context** is also shaped by other factors, including social, historical, cultural, political and environmental influences.

1.1.1: Warm-up

Who am I?

Complete the graphic with some information about your personal context.

When you are finished, share your graphic with a peer. Discuss any similarities you both share and talk about what makes you unique.

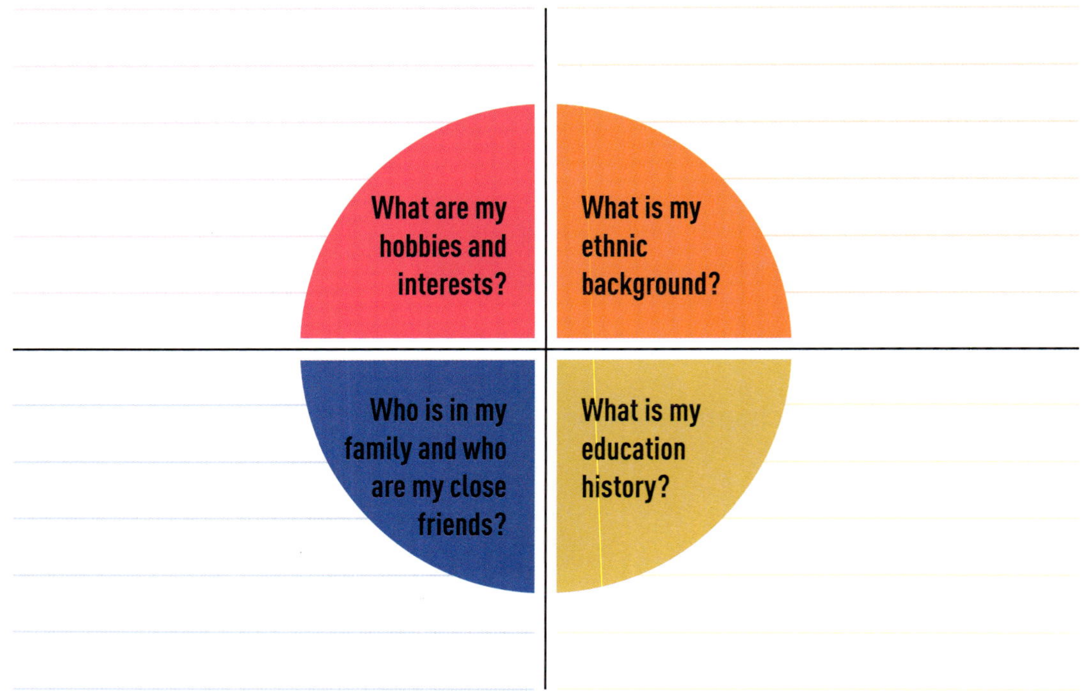

1.1.2: Reading texts

Texts such as **memoirs** and **autobiographies** are one way of sharing our personal context with the world. The following extract is from Jessica Watson's autobiography *True Spirit*. Australian Watson was 16 years old when she became the youngest person to sail solo and unassisted around the world. Consider how Watson's personal context influenced her identity and aspirations.

> **VOCABULARY**
>
> **Autobiography**
> *noun* an account of a person's life written by that person.
>
> **Memoir**
> *noun* a narrative, written from the point of view of the author, about an important part of their life.

> **LANGUAGE**
>
> An autobiography is written in the **first person**. How does Watson use of the first person help us understand her context better?

True Spirit

By Jessica Watson

Living on the water on the family's motorboat, surrounded by all things nautical, meant sailing and boating had become a big part of my life. But until the day Mum started to read us Jesse Martin's *Lionheart*, I'd never even considered that I could one day become an adventurer. I'd always thought of adventurers as grey-haired men with beards who climbed mountains or flew old aeroplanes across wide expanses of ocean. Hearing about Jesse made me think differently. It was as if something clicked in my mind. This guy wasn't a superhero, he wasn't privileged in any way, he didn't have a beard and he definitely wasn't old. Jesse was a normal, everyday person who had a dream and decided to make it happen. He was someone I could relate to and it made me wonder ... could I do it? Could I sail around the world on my own?

I didn't tell anyone at first what was going through my head. I started reading everything I could about solo sailing. I made lists of what I'd need and collected articles about boats and rigging and long-lasting food. Mum says she knew something was going on because I started putting pictures of huge Southern Ocean waves and storms above my berth. I was visualising myself dealing with the wild seas and fierce winds before I even knew what visualisation was ...

My parents had always encouraged me to dream and, with their help, I was going to do everything I could to make my dream come true. Thanks to sailors like Jesse Martin, Kay Cottee, David Dicks and Tania Aebi I knew that normal people could do extraordinary things. I wanted to be one of them.

1 Explain how each aspect of Watson's personal context influenced her dream to sail solo around the world.

Personal context	How did this influence her dream?
Family	
Hobbies and/or Interests	

2 Describe Watson's personal identity. What beliefs and values are important to her?

1.1.3: Reading reflection

Jessica Watson's goal was heavily influenced by reading Jesse Martin's ***Lionheart.*** (**Optional:** *Use the QR code to access information about Jesse Martin for further reading about his personal context.)*

1 Describe a time when you have been influenced by something you have read.

1.1.4 Understanding and responding to texts B

Reading about other people's experiences can help us understand how others live and how their personal contexts are similar or different to ours. The next text you will read is an extract from Deng Thiak Adut's memoir *Songs of a War Boy,* in which he shares his experience of fleeing South Sudan as a refugee and arriving in Australia.

Songs of a War Boy

By Deng Thiak Adut

The SPLA (Sudanese People's Liberation Army) would build an army of war boys. I would be a part of that army. I would be a war boy.

I remember how I spent my last day as a civilian – I

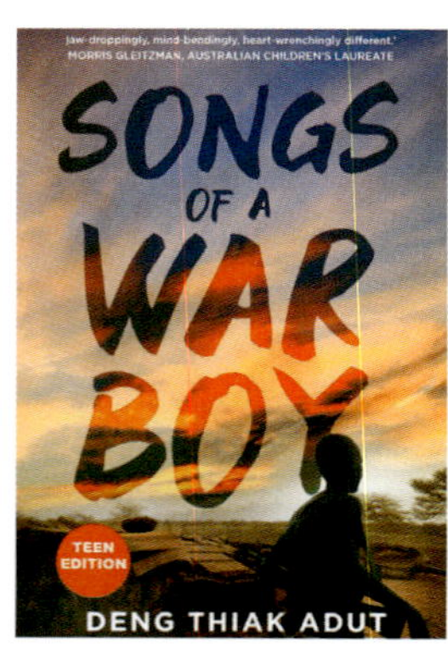

played at being a man ...

When my camp was finished, I would move the mud cows around and imagine all the sons that would be working for me. I'd also compose the songs that would be written about my life – songs of hunting and fishing, wrestling and cow-herding, songs about tall wives, and strong sons.

There would be no songs for me, however, because that would be the last day I would spend in my village as a villager.

That was the day that I fell off the edge of the world of children, and landed in another world. I did not land in the world of men though – the world I yearned to be part of – but another world. In this world there was no family, and no gods, no Nile eagles and no Nhialic. In this new world there was only one thing: the machine that is war.

I was destined to be a useful part of that machine, or I was destined to be dead. I was no longer Little Swallow, or the God Eater, or even Deng Adut. I was SPLA. I would be that or I would be nothing.

On that day I was seven years old.

CONTEXT

Deng Thiak Adut was born in South Sudan in 1983, the same year that the Second Sudanese Civil War started.

LANGUAGE

A **metaphor** is a figurative expression in which words mean something different than their literal interpretation.

Look closely at the paragraph that starts *'That was the day...'*. Underline the metaphor and discuss with a peer why Adut uses this comparison.

1 How did the war impact Adut's childhood?

____

____

____

2 How do you think Adut's experiences as a child might have influenced his opinion on war and the impact it has on children?

____

____

____

3 How do you feel after reading about Adut's experience?

____

____

____

What is a perspective and how do texts share them?

A **perspective** is a lens through which we see the world. The way we see the world is influenced heavily by our personal context and what we believe is important. When we read a text we bring our own context and experiences, which position us to see the writer's message in certain way. However, a writer is also influenced by their own context in the creation of a text and they use this text to share their own **perspective** on the topic.

We will now examine texts and consider what **perspective** they share with the world.

1.1.5 Understanding and responding to texts B

Look closely at the front cover image of Turia Pitt's non-fiction book *Happy (and other ridiculous aspirations)*. In this book Pitt shares her interviews with a range of well-known people about what it means to be happy.

Turia Pitt is an Australian motivational speaker. At age 24 she was trapped in a grass fire and suffered burns to 65 per cent of her body. She has endured over 200 surgeries and is known for her determination.

1 From what you have read about Pitt's personal context and the image of her on the book, what do you think is her **perspective** about life after injury?

___

___

___

2 How does the design of the book cover support your idea about Pitt's **perspective**?

___

___

___

1.1.6 Understanding and responding to texts B

The next text is an open letter written by Wiradjuri man Stan Grant to his sons, published in *The Sydney Morning Herald.*

PAUSE AND DISCUSS: Before you read this text, talk with your peers about what you know about the historical, social and political context of Aboriginal and Torres Strait Islander peoples in Australia.

The lessons Stan Grant hopes to pass onto his sons

By Stan Grant (5 September 2021)

Your Pop has given you the most wonderful gift. He has given you our language. Because of him, Wiradjuri is protected and preserved forever. He's written it all down in the Wiradjuri dictionary. A whole generation of people speak our language now because your Pop saved it. That's what keeps him alive. That's what the Garru said to him when he was sick. It wasn't his time yet.

But we are losing him. I know we won't have him forever. And I'm scared, boys. I am scared because I'm not ready. I am scared because I'm not man enough yet to live without him in the world. I need him to fight just a bit longer to give me time to grow.

When he is gone, I will have to take his place. I will have to plant my feet in our soil and pull all of our strength from the earth. I will have to stand under the stars and speak to Baiame to ask him to make me a man.

We spend our lives preparing for this, my boys. Remember when you were young and we would drive from Sydney to Nan and Pop's house? Remember those long drives? We used to stop at Yass to get petrol and have lunch, not just for the food but because it marked the start of Wiradjuri Country: your Country.

Remember how I told you about the land? You would look at the rocks and the hills. I told you how the land dipped into a valley and rose on the other

LANGUAGE

Tick the language features you can see used in the text:

- ◯ Aboriginal and/or Torres Strait Islander languages
- ◯ Inclusive language
- ◯ Rhetorical question
- ◯ Repetition
- ◯ Metaphor
- ◯ Anecdote

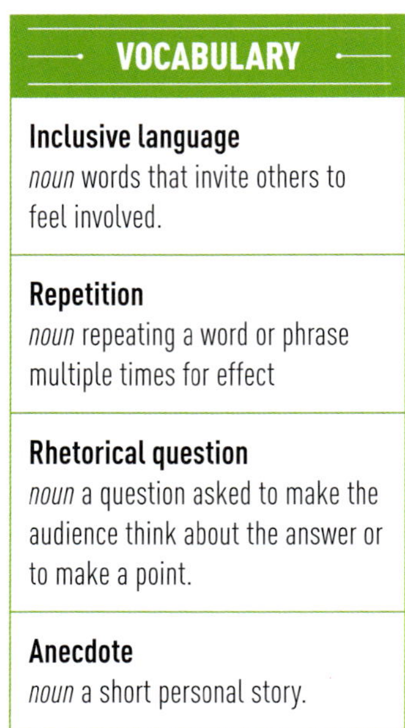

VOCABULARY

Inclusive language
noun words that invite others to feel involved.

Repetition
noun repeating a word or phrase multiple times for effect

Rhetorical question
noun a question asked to make the audience think about the answer or to make a point.

Anecdote
noun a short personal story.

side: that side was home. You watched how the sun hit the trees and how the earth flattened out and how creeks cut across it like blood veins.

Home, boys. You have only one home in the entire world. One home that has always been there and will always be there. One home and a family: our blood in our Country.

Love, Dad.

1 In his letter, Grant shares his perspectives on important issues. Complete the table below.

Issue	What is Grant's perspective on this issue? Give an example.
Wiradjuri language	
Family	
The Australian land	

2 The letter is addressed to Grant's sons but is really written for a broader audience. Who is this audience and why do you think Grant wants to share his perspective about his culture with them?

3 Grant's letter has a very personal voice. Circle one of the words below that could be used to describe his voice in this letter.

Passionate **Concerned** **Inspirational**

a. Write down an example of his personal voice from the text.

___

___

___

b. How does this personal voice connect with one of Grant's perspectives shared in the text?

___

___

___

How can I share a personal experience in a text of my own, inspired by my reading experiences?

You have read about the personal contexts, experiences and perspectives of others and now you will share an aspect of your personal experience in a text of your own.

1.1.7 Expressing ideas and composing texts A and B 

1 Choose one of the prompts below and write a personal composition about your experience:

- a time when you showed bravery
- a lesson learned from a mistake
- a moment that turned out to be better than expected.

Your writing should be inspired by your reading experiences in this chapter.

2 Select a **FORM** and inspiration for your composition:

- ☐ Autobiography extract (Jessica Watson, *True Spirit*)
- ☐ Memoir extract (Deng Thiak Adut, *Songs of a War Boy*)
- ☐ Open letter (Stan Grant, *The lessons Stan Grant hopes to pass onto his sons*)

3 Circle two **LANGUAGE FEATURES** you will use in your response, as inspired by the text extracts in this chapter.

First-Person Language	Inclusive Language	Rhetorical Question
Metaphor	Anecdote	Repetition

4 Now, combine these choices and write about this personal experience:

1.1.8 Chapter reflection

In this chapter, we have examined how texts can reflect who we are; our **personal context** and our **perspectives.**

1 Summarise your understanding of these key vocabulary terms of this unit and identify a text in the chapter that developed this knowledge.

Vocabulary term	Your understanding	Text from Chapter 1
Context		
Perspective		

The texts examined in this chapter each provide a different **perspective** on an aspect of the human experience.

2 Summarise the perspective shared by each text.

Text	Focus	Perspective
Jessica Watson, *True Spirit*	Goals and Aspirations	
Deng Thiak Adut, *Songs of a War Boy*	Childhood and War	
Turia Pitt, *Happy (and other ridiculous aspirations)*	Happiness after adversity (challenge)	
Stan Grant *The lessons Stan Grant hopes to pass onto his sons*	Aboriginal and Torres Strait Islander culture	

3 The texts we examined in this chapter were written in different forms (autobiography, memoir, book cover and letter). Which text form did you enjoy studying the most and why?

4 Let's return to the inquiry question: ***How can texts share who we are and what is most important to us?*** How have your reading experiences in Chapter 1 addressed this inquiry question?

CHAPTER 2

TEXTS THAT PERSUADE

Chapter overview

In the first chapter, you learned about how texts can reflect who we are and our perspectives. In this chapter you will further this learning by exploring how texts can use these perspectives and personal voice to create a persuasive argument about issues of importance in our world.

You will examine texts such as opinion pieces and speeches, and make connections between the texts in the way they use similar forms, features, structures and themes to create an argument.

Success criteria: In this chapter, I will be successful when I can ...

- describe the purpose of a persuasive text
- identify features of a persuasive text
- identify the position presented in a persuasive text
- explain how personal voice is used in persuasive texts to create an argument
- compare how persuasive texts use similar forms, features, structures and themes to create an argument
- evaluate the effectiveness of forms and features within persuasive texts to shape audience response.

Chapter inquiry questions

- What is a persuasive text?
- How do texts use personal voice to present an argument?
- How can I compare persuasive texts with similar forms and features?

Key vocabulary

- Persuasive
- Argument
- Personal voice

What is a persuasive text?

A persuasive text is created to convince a reader or an audience of a particular opinion on an issue. The writer of a persuasive text firstly presents a position or a certain view or opinion on this issue. The writer then uses a range of features throughout the text to make readers think in a similar way or take a certain action.

1.2.1 Warm-up

Would you rather?

1 With a small group, discuss your responses to each of the questions below. Give reasons for your choices.

be able to fly	OR	be invisible?
have only Winter as a season	OR	have only Summer as a season?
be able to pause moments in your life	OR	be able to rewind to moments in the past?
have no internet for a month	OR	have no shower or bath for a month?
live in a world without hate	OR	live in a world without hunger?

2 Now, choose one of your responses from above. For your response, list three reasons in the space below to support your choice.

i. ______________________________

ii. ______________________________

iii. ______________________________

1.2.2 Reading reflection

1 You see persuasive texts every day, whether you are aware of them or not. Have a look at these posters that encourage others to look after our environment. Under each poster, write one reason why it is persuasive.

2 Which poster do you think is most effective at convincing others to look after the planet? Explain your choice with reference to specific parts of the poster.

Speeches

One type of persuasive text that you will examine in this chapter is a speech. You may have heard a persuasive speech during assembly or on television, or you may even have even written one yourself. Speeches can be very persuasive as they use written language features to influence the audience, such as inclusive language, repetition, rhetorical questions and emotive language.

1.2.3 Reading texts

A speaker can also make the speech persuasive by the way they present it, such as using emphasis, pause, pace and gestures. You will now examine Dylan Alcott's 2022 Australian of the Year speech as an example of a persuasive speech.

Dylan Alcott's 2022 Australian of the Year speech

I love my disability. It is the best thing that ever happened to me. It really is and I'm so thankful for the life that I get to live...

But I know that for the 4.5 million people in this country, one in five people that have a physical or non-physical disability, they don't feel the same way that I do and it's not their fault.

But it's up to all of us to do things so that they can get out and be proud of their disability as well and be the people that they want to be.

We've got to fund the NDIS [National Disability Insurance Scheme], first and foremost and listen to people with lived experience and ask them what they need ...

We've got to keep improving more employment opportunities for people with a disability as well. Of those 4.5 million people, only 54 per cent of them are involved in the workforce. The unemployment rate is double that of able-bodied people. Both figures haven't moved in 30 years.

And, guess what? We're not just ready to work, we're ready to take your jobs, alright? We are coming ! We are coming! But we've got to get those opportunities. And lastly, we have to have greater representation of people with a disability absolutely everywhere. In our boardrooms, in our parliaments, in our mainstream schools, on our dating apps, on our sporting fields, in our universities, absolutely everywhere, so we get the opportunity to start living our lives just like everyone else and I promise you, you won't just enrich the lives of us, but also yourselves in the process.

CONTEXT

Dylan Alcott is a former wheelchair tennis player who has represented Australia at four Paralympic Games.

INTERPRET

Underline one section of the text that you think sounds the most convincing. Compare with a peer and discuss what you each chose.

Scan the QR code to view the full speech.

1 What is the purpose of Alcott's speech? Start your sentence with: The purpose of Alcott's speech is to ...

____

____

____

2 Who is the audience of Alcott's speech? Give some evidence to support your answer.

____

____

____

3 List two phrases that Alcott says that you think are persuasive. Explain why each phrase is persuasive in convincing the audience of his message. (Remember, when you quote directly from the speech you must use quotation marks.)

Phrase from speech	Why is this phrase persuasive?

Opinion pieces

Another type of persuasive text is an opinion piece. An opinion piece is usually published in a newspaper, magazine or journal and shares the author's opinion on a particular topic. This type of text may read more like a conversation but it may also use evidence, such as studies or statistics, to support the writer's opinion. As you read an opinion piece you will be positioned to see the writer's point of view.

VOCABULARY

Position
noun The writer's overall stance or opinion on a topic.

verb The way a reader is made to see a topic using text structure and language.

1.2.4 Reading texts

An example of an opinion piece is the following article 'Is 13 too young to have a TikTok or Instagram account?', by Catherine Page Jeffery, published in *The Conversation*.

Use the QR code to access and read the article.

1 What is the Jeffery's opinion on the topic of a minimum age for social media accounts?

2 The article uses subheadings throughout the text to help position the reader. Choose and list three subheadings in the table below and explain how each section of text adds to the Jeffery's opinion.

Subheading	How does this section of text add to the writer's opinion?

1.2.5 Reading reflection

Reflect on this article from your viewpoint as a teenager. What would you say to adults who are concerned about the minimum age for having a social media account? Share your opinion persuasively.

How do texts use personal voice to present an argument?

A key part of any persuasive text is its argument or the writer's position on a certain topic. While you may think of argument in terms of conflict, yelling or screaming, an argument in writing doesn't need to be combative. Instead, writers create an argument by using various elements of a text (including theme, perspective and style) to represent their opinion. This means that when you write, you need to plan your response carefully to build your argument over the course of the text.

1.2.6 Understanding and responding to texts B

Let's look at an example of argument that is not combative and that uses various elements to construct and maintain the writer's position.

I call Australia home now, but I feel lucky that I've held onto my culture

By Shayan, ABC Heywire 8 December 2022

...When we moved from Iran to Wagga Wagga five years ago, it was difficult to make conversations and talk the way I used to — so freely and easily in Persian, without needing to concentrate too much and be anxious.

English isn't my first language, and not knowing it created uncertainties in my mind, like "How I will make friends", "What will school be like?"

Lunch and recess were hard at first. It felt lonely at times.

... As my English improved, things changed. I started getting excited about different subjects at school. I love modern history. I've realised how important Persian cultural history and language are to my identity.

... When I get home from school, I only speak Persian with my parents. As we talk, there's a flow to the language that is hard to describe. I feel like I can just go on and on in Persian.

It feels different when I'm speaking English to a friend; not only because it's a different language but because it's two different cultures and worlds. I live in both.

...I think those from different backgrounds, especially in rural areas, should keep learning and not forget their first language, as it shapes a massive part of them.

Post-migration people tend to let this valuable asset slip away, especially in rural areas with less diversity and opportunities for communication in different languages.

I won't forget my first language. I'm going to keep expressing myself in Persian — it's part of me.

LANGUAGE

In Chapter 1, you learned that an anecdote is a short personal story. Underline examples of anecdote in this opinion piece.

INTERPRET

Circle a section of the text that you think reveals Shayan's main argument.

1 What is Shayan's argument about culture and language?

2 How does Shayan's use of personal anecdotes add to his argument? Refer to one anecdote as an example.

3 The argument in this article is not presented combatively or aggressively, but it is still persuasive. Do you agree or disagree? Give evidence from the article to support your reasoning.

1.2.7 Reading reflection

The opinion piece 'I call Australia home now…' offers a unique perspective on the struggles of migrants arriving in Australia. What other groups of people also face challenges in our society? Complete this Claim, Support, Question thinking routine below in a small group to create your own perspectives on this topic.

Claim	Given an opinion about a group of people in Australia who face challenges in our society
Support	Support your claim with your own experiences (things you have witnessed, read, viewed, felt, etc.)
Question	Ask questions related to each other's claims. For example: Is this claim true because …? What has happened to cause …? What could be done to help …?

Journal your thoughts at the conclusion of your discussion. What new thoughts do you have to add to your initial perspective?

____

____

____

____

____

VOCABULARY

Tone
noun The attitude of the writer towards the topic, often described by words associated with emotions. For example: optimistic tone, reflective tone, sarcastic tone.

Building an argument in a written persuasive text is also achieved through the writer's use of personal voice. In writing, 'voice' refers to the unique style of a writer. The way a writer uses specific words and types of sentences creates voice. A writer's voice often sets the tone for a text and can shape the way you respond to the text, including how you are persuaded to agree with their opinion.

Sharing personal experiences in texts, as we examined in Chapter 1, is one way that the writer may create voice to help build an argument in a written text. Sharing these experiences may influence the reader to feel sympathetic or may even add credibility to their argument if the writer has first-hand experience of the topic.

1.2.8 Understanding and responding to texts B

The next text you will examine is 'Forever Fixing' by El Gibbs, from the anthology *Growing up Disabled in Australia* edited by. Carly Findlay. The text shares Gibbs's personal experience with psoriasis, an immune system disorder characterised by a rash on the skin, and arthritis, inflammation of one or more joints.

Forever Fixing

By El Gibbs

No one told me when I first got sick that I had abruptly joined a community, one with a history, and theories, and ways of being. Instead, I was told to relentlessly search for a cure, and an exit, no matter the cost — to wage war on my diseased self. I had become disabled — not just by my disease, but by the way the world treated me. When I found out, everything changed.

PREDICT

With a peer, discuss what you predict the writer's argument might be. When you finish reading, come back to your predictions and see what you got right.

*

It all started with a few spots on my arm one summer day. A few red, flaky spots that I ignored... But the spots had their own agenda. They joined together and spread down my arm, and then all over my body. Various doctors peered at me and pronounced that it was nothing to worry about. 'Here is a cream that will fix you.' Three months later, I was covered from head to toe in crimson, weepy, flaking, hot, sore skin. It cracked every time I breathed in or out, and I bled on everything. By now, the doctors had agreed that a cream probably wouldn't fix me and that I had to go to hospital. For a few days, right? No, they said. For a few weeks. I was nineteen.

*

... The medical model of disability says that I am broken because my body has a disease, and it doesn't work the way a so-called 'normal' body does. There is this normal body, you see, that doctors learn about, described in medical textbooks. When things go wrong with this fictional body, medicine is applied, and the body returns to its normal state. All better now.

INTERPRET

With a peer, describe the Gibbs's voice in Paragraph three. Why do you think she sounds this way after her medical experience?

*

... The social model of disability gave me a framework for understanding my chronic illness, but it sometimes had little room for my actual experience of being sick... That I had to focus on finding a cure? What did it mean if I decided not to try any more treatments? What would happen when there were no more treatments to try?

*

... I now understand myself as a disabled person, and the disabled life that I live... I wish I could tell that isolated terrified teen – sitting on the hospital fire escape, sobbing and feeling so alone – that one day she won't feel that way. She will find a place in the world where every part of her belongs, and where there is no need to hide. And she can do this while still being sick, still being sore and still looking different.

LANGUAGE

In the last paragraph, the writer uses a strong, reassuring voice. Circle words or phrases that help to create this voice.

1 What is Gibbs's argument about disability?

2 How has Gibbs's personal context shaped her perspective of disability and inclusion?

3 There are several audiences that Gibbs may be addressing in this text. What does Gibbs hope to convince each audience about disability? Find evidence to support your ideas.

Audience	What does Gibbs want to convince this audience of?	Evidence from text
Disabled community		
Non-disabled community		

4 Gibbs uses a different tone in various sections of the text to control her overall argument. Identify one tone that she uses in a particular section of the text and explain how this adds to her argument. Remember to use quotation marks when you quote from the text.

Extension activity

An em dash is a type of punctuation that is used to add additional information to a sentence, such as examples, explanations or descriptions.

Gibbs uses a few em dashes in her writing. For example, 'I had become disabled – not just by my disease, but by the way the world treated me' uses an em dash to add that she was not disabled by her physical condition alone, but instead disabled by the way the world treated her and excluded her.

Another em dash is used in the final paragraph. Can you find it? Discuss with a peer why the em dash is used here.

You may consider using an em dash during your next writing response.

How can I compare persuasive texts with similar forms and features?

Now that you understand the purpose of persuasive texts and the way they use voice to create an argument, let's explore how writers create persuasive language through similar forms and features. Persuasive language can help to construct and maintain an argument. Remember, not all persuasive texts need to be forceful in their tone. Instead, persuasion may be achieved through other **rhetorical devices** that appeal to and engage the audience.

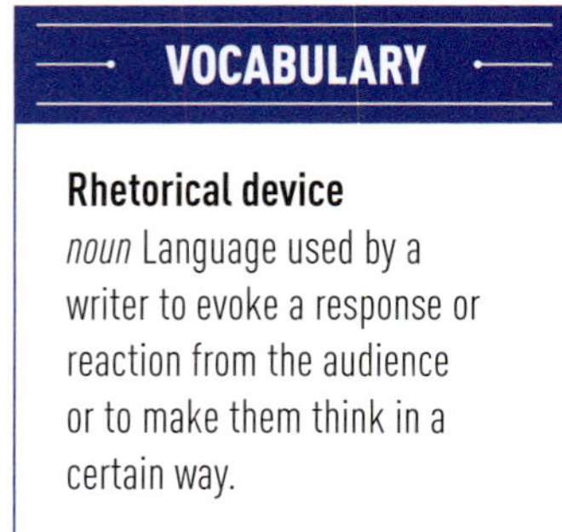

Here are some common persuasive language features.

Feature	Definition	Example
Rhetorical question	A question that is asked not because the asker is expecting an answer, but to emphasise a point or to make people think	'What child, taken away from the care of his or her parents, will not suffer some form of psychological trauma?'

Write a rhetorical question that you could use if you were trying to persuade someone to clean the school grounds.

Feature	Definition	Example
Emotive language	Deliberately strong words used to provoke emotion	'illiterate, penniless teenager, traumatised physically and emotionally'

Using emotive language, write two sentences someone could use to persuade their parents to let them go to a party.

Feature	Definition	Example
Inclusive language	Words such as 'we', 'our' or 'us', used to make listeners feel included	'how very lucky we are'

You are the coach of a sports team. Write the first sentence of your halftime speech to the team to motivate them to play better together.

Feature	Definition	Example
Repetition	Repeating words, phrases or ideas for emphasis	'I lost ...'

Find a real-life example of a text that uses repetition for emphasis, such as a line from an advertising jingle or a song lyric.

Feature	Definition	Example
Imperative	To give a command or direct instruction to the audience	'Stop waiting! Act now! It's time to help our planet'

Find or invent a news article headline or advertisement that uses an imperative to instruct readers.

Feature	Definition	Example
Anecdote	A short personal story included to illustrate or support a point	'My earliest memory of getting sunburnt was in primary school. It was a Friday in the middle of summer ...'

Use an anecdote from your experience of learning from home to persuade your school principal to make learning from home happen one day each week.

Now that you have learned what these persuasive features are called, think back to the texts you have read in this chapter. Choose one text you have previously read and label the persuasive features used.

1.2.9 Expressing ideas and composing texts

1 Write a paragraph to compare two texts examined in this chapter use similar persuasive features to create and control an argument.

Remember to provide textual evidence and use quotation marks for direct quotes from any of the texts.

When you compare the texts, try to use some of the example comparative words or phrases below.

Similarly	Likewise	In the same way
On the other hand	However	Alternatively

1.2.10 Chapter reflection

In this chapter, we have examined how texts use persuasive features to create an argument about issues of importance.

Summarise your understanding of the key vocabulary of this chapter.

Vocabulary Term	Your Understanding
Persuasive	
Argument	
Personal Voice	

The texts you have read in this chapter touch on very important issues in our world today. You would have read or viewed texts about these same issues previously. For each of the texts and issues listed below, list another text you have read or viewed that you feel connects in some way.

Text	Issue	Similar Text I've Read or Viewed
Dylan Alcott, Australian of the Year Speech	Disability Awareness	
Catherine Page Jeffery, Is 13 too young to have a Tiktok account?	Social Media	
Shayan, I call Australia home now...	Culture and Language	
El Gibbs, Forever Fixing	Disability and Inclusion	

Let's return to the inquiry question: ***How can texts share who we are and what is most important to us?*** How have your reading experiences in this chapter addressed the inquiry question?

___

___

___

___

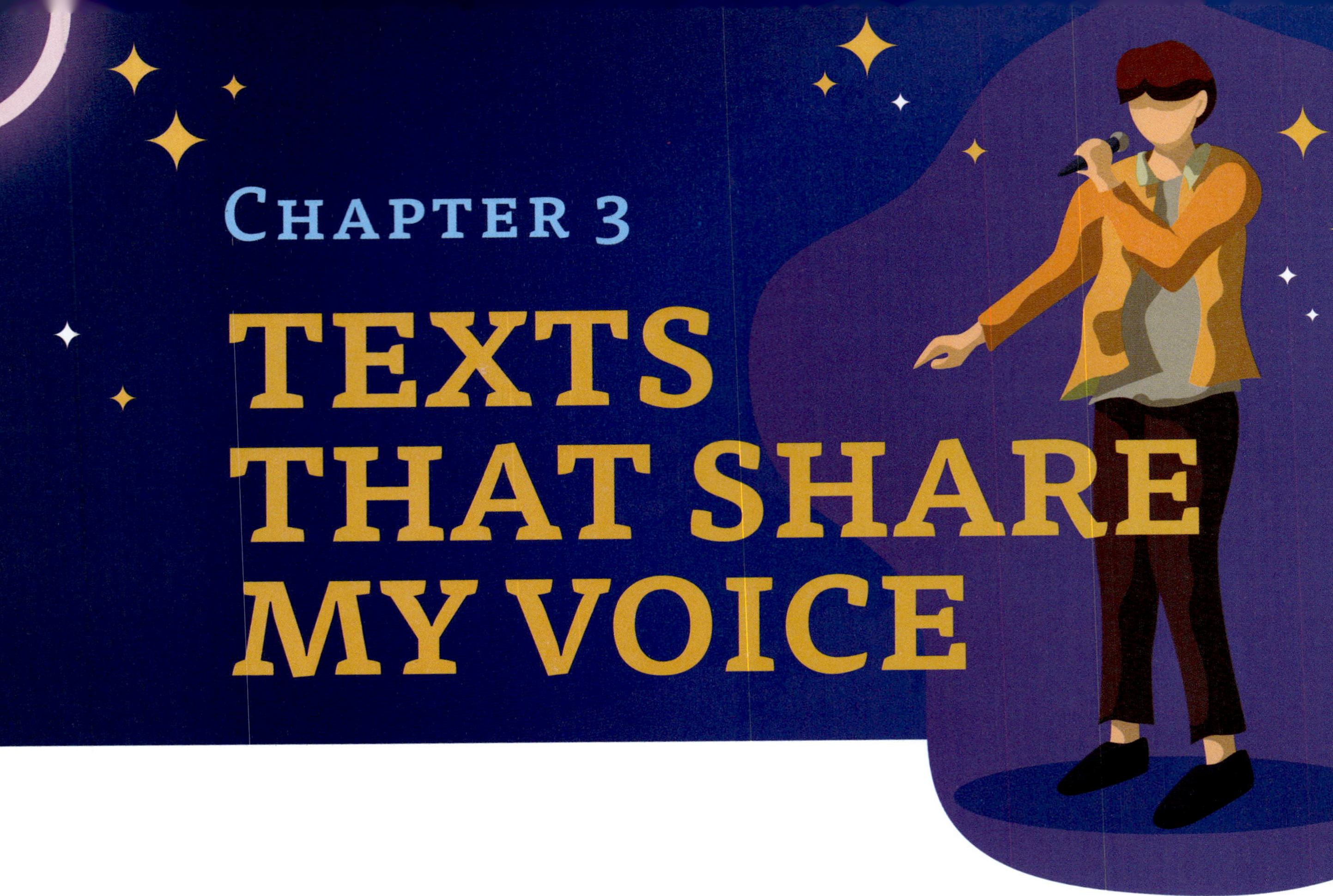

Chapter overview

You have learned about how texts can share personal experiences and perspectives and turn these into an argument using personal voice. Now you will make your own personal connections with the world as you consider what issues are most important to you, inspired by your reading experiences and personal values.

You will consider the issues raised in the texts examined in this unit, plus others from your own reading. You will also experiment with some of the language forms and features of persuasive writing to share your own arguments.

Success criteria: In this chapter, I will be successful when I can ...

- describe my personal values and perspectives
- identify important issues in our contemporary world
- explain why these issues are important to me
- plan the language and structural choices of my writing, inspired by my reading
- present my own arguments about issues of importance to me using persuasive language features.

Chapter inquiry questions

- What do I value in the world right now?
- What perspectives do I have about what is important in the world?
- How can I use persuasive writing to share my perspectives?

Key vocabulary

- Values
- Issue
- Contemporary

What do I value in the world right now?

What is a value?

A **value** is a principle or core belief that you hold with great importance. Values often guide our choices and the way we act. For example, if you believe that honesty is an important value, this will influence the way you act with your friends and the way you expect to be treated. Your values have been formed over time – this could be a result of significant experiences, your relationships with people in your life or your involvement in community groups. Your teenage years are full of experiences that will challenge your values to help you better understand what is important to you.

1.3.1 Warm-up

What does the world need right now?

Group activity: Examine the list of values below. Your whole team must agree on only five values that our world needs right now to become a better place. Each person must give their opinion and explain their reasoning before you decide on your final five values.

Fairness	Family	Selflessness	Honesty
Love	Equality	Acceptance	Truth
Respect	Bravery	Loyalty	Spirituality
Community	Justice	Simplicity	Gratitude

Individual Activity: Journal your individual thoughts after the group activity. Did others agree with your opinion? Did your team struggle to decide unanimously? What did this experience reveal about what values are most important for you personally?

1.3.2 Reading reflection

1 Have a look at these quotes from some of the texts we examined in this unit. What does each quote suggest about what the writer values? Use the list of values in the warm-up activity to help guide your response.

Quote	What does this quote suggest about what the writer values?
'You have only one home in the entire world. One home that has always been there and will always be there. One home and a family: our blood in our Country.' Stan Grant (Chapter 1)	
'She will find a place in the world where every part of her belongs, and where there is no need to hide.' El Gibbs (Chapter 2)	

2 This chapter will help you better understand what you value so that you can share your perspectives on issues of importance in our world.

But first, what do you value in the world right now? Journal your initial thoughts with explanation. Use the list of values in the warm-up activity if you need inspiration.

Films

In this unit we have looked at how opinions and values are shared via autobiographies, memoirs, speeches and opinion articles. Another text that can share issues of importance is a film. Films are often created to target the interests and needs of the audience, and therefore reflect issues we are currently thinking about or feel are important.

1.3.3 Reading texts

You will now read an extract of a review of Ang Lee's film *Life of Pi* that connects a key setting of the film to the issue of climate change.

Life of Pi's acidic island a warning for our warming world

By Thomas Faunce, The Conversation, *27 January 2013*

The recently released film *Life of Pi* directed by Ang Lee and based on Yann Martel's novel of the same name, is a fable for our climate change times. Much of the plot involves the struggles of a teenage boy named 'Pi' Patel, trying to survive a shipwreck in which his family dies ... Pi becomes stranded in the Pacific Ocean on a lifeboat with a tiger named Richard Parker. ...

After many trials, Pi and Richard Parker reach a strange island made of plants that Pi eats. It has a forest, fresh water pools, and a large population of meerkats that sustain Richard Parker. At night, however, the meerkats flee to the trees and Richard Parker to the lifeboat.

Pi watches from a branch as the island's fresh water turns acidic, digesting fish that have died in the pools. ...

Castello Aragonese is a small island which really exists in the Tyrrhenian Sea near Naples. Bubbles of carbon dioxide rise from volcanic vents on the seafloor and dissolve to form high concentrations of carbonic acid that make seawater corrosive... no other life survives in its waters. All the world's oceans are predicted to become this acidified

by 2100 with severe impacts on small lifeforms in the ocean. ...

Even if our carbon emissions were stabilised today, it would take tens of thousands of years for ocean pH to return to normal. Coral reefs and the small creatures that sustain the food chain for whales, for example, would perish, the oceans will become so corrosive (like those of the waters around Pi's island) that the shells of many small sea creatures will simply dissolve.

The acidic island of the *Life of Pi* film contains a subtle, artistic warning for humanity.

VOCABULARY

Corrosive
adjective capable of destroying solid objects, tending to eat away or consume.

LANGUAGE

Underline all examples of scientific language (jargon) that help give credibility to this argument.

Scan the QR code to view the full review.

1 What is unique about the island in the film *Life of Pi* that Faunce refers to?

____

____

2 What connection is Faunce making between the film and an issue in our world or a value that the world needs to consider?

____

____

____

3 How does Faunce's use of scientific language (jargon) help to give credibility to this discussion? Give examples from the text.

____

____

____

4 What action do you think Faunce wants the audience to take after reading this review?

____

____

____

____

1.3.4 Expressing ideas and composing texts A and B

Choose a film you have viewed that you think reveals an issue or important value and write a brief review connecting the film to the issue we need to consider.

Here are some films you may have seen that could inspire your thinking.

> **VOCABULARY**
>
> **Issue**
> *noun* an important topic or problem for debate or discussion.

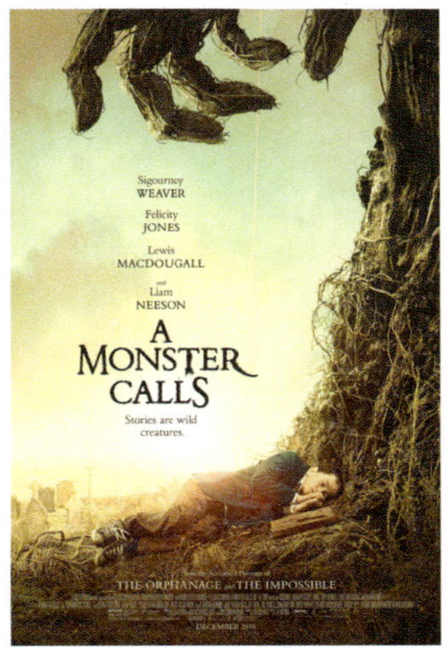

Before you write, you must always plan your ideas to help build your argument. Use these planning tools to guide your organisation.

Film title: ______________________________

Director: ______________________________

Values – What values does the film make you think about? Are these values that you have too?	
Identities – Who is the intended audience of the film? Why does this audience need to know about this issue?	
Actions – What action does the film want the audience to take regarding this issue?	

You must also plan the language and structural choices you will make to write your text. Use this checklist to help you plan. Tick the features you plan to use to build your argument.

Feature	Inspiration text/s and chapter	Tick (if you want to use this)
Inclusive language to involve your audience	'The lessons Stan Grant hopes to pass onto his sons' (Chapter 1)	
Subheadings to structure your argument	'Is 13 too young to have a TikTok or Instagram account?' (Chapter 2)	
Anecdote to connect to your own experiences	'I call Australia home now' (Chapter 2) 'Forever Fixing' (Chapter 2)	
Jargon or language related to the issue	*Life of Pi* film review (Chapter 3)	

Now it is time to write your film review.

What perspectives do I have about what is important in the world?

Throughout this unit you have read about the experiences of others in the world. It is now time to consider your own perspectives on important issues.

1.3.5 Understanding and responding to texts B

Choose a writer you have encountered in any of the chapters in this unit, or another writer or character you have come across in your own reading. Complete the 'Same, Different, Connect, Engage' activity to consider how you might connect to their experience of the world.

Writer/character: ____________________

Text: ____________________

Same – In what ways might this person and you have similar values?	
Different – In what ways might this person and you have different values?	
Connect – In what ways might this person and you be connected as human beings in the world?	
Engage – What would you like to ask, say to or do with this person if you had the chance?	

Now that you have connected with this writer or character and their experience, it is time to consider how this reading experience has broadened your perspective of the world and issues of importance. Using the same text and person as above, complete the following activity to develop a personal perspective of your own.

Issue – What is the main issue represented in this text?	
Perspective – What is my perspective on this issue? What is my opinion or position?	

Audience – Who do I think needs to know about this issue in our world right now?	
Intent – What change do I want to see in the world regarding this issue? What action do I want the audience to take?	

1.3.6 Expressing ideas and composing texts A and B

You will now write the opening of an opinion piece to share your perspective on the issue you have identified as one of importance for you.

You must focus on using a **personal voice** to convey your perspective and you must consider how you will use **tone** to create this voice.

1 Go back to Chapter 2 to refresh your memory of the purpose and features of an opinion piece as well as how to create voice through written tone.

2 Plan the tone you wish to use in your opinion piece opening. Here are some words that may inspire the tone you wish to use.

Serious	Inspirational	Reflective	Light-hearted
Cautionary	Humorous	Informal	Critical

I plan to use a tone that is

____

I have chosen this tone because

____

____

One text that I have read that uses this tone is

____

____

3 Write the opening to your opinion article here. Remember to include a title for your article that gives a preview of the issue you will discuss or your perspective on this issue.

Extension activity

Dash

Some of the writers we have examined in this unit have used the punctuation feature of a dash to create and control their voice. Go back to Chapter 2 for a reminder of the purpose and use of an em dash. Challenge yourself to use this in your response.

How can I use persuasive writing to share my perspectives?

You have started to develop your own perspective on an issue that is important to you and for our contemporary world. You will now further this by learning how to build an argument around this perspective and share your view persuasively.

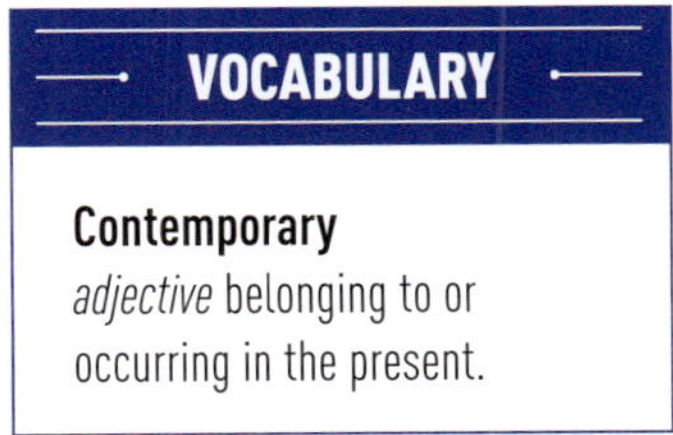

VOCABULARY

Contemporary
adjective belonging to or occurring in the present.

In this unit, you have learned that a text can persuade an audience by ...

- presenting a position on a topic or issue
- building an argument through the logical sequencing of ideas
- using a personal voice to connect readers to the main idea
- employing a range of persuasive language features to creatively influence an audience.

1.3.7 Expressing ideas and composing texts A and B

The United Nations Youth Australia's National Conference is an event for young people aged 12 to 25 to discuss issues that they feel are most important. Imagine you have been invited to this event.

Write a section of a speech to deliver at this conference that persuasively shares an argument about one issue you feel is important for Australia's youth right now. Be inspired by the speech you have read in this unit by Dylan Alcott (Chapter 2).

1 Plan the **logical sequencing of ideas** to build your argument. Use this tool to plan.

Issue: ______________________________

My position: ______________________________

Aim of speech: ______________________________

IDEA 1

IDEA 2

IDEA 3

2 Tick <u>three</u> persuasive language features from this table that you will use in your speech extract to convince the audience of your argument. Identify texts from this unit that have used these features effectively to convince their audience.

Feature	Text/s that used this feature effectively	Tick (if you want to use this)
Rhetorical question		
Emotive language		
Inclusive language		
Repetition		
Imperative		
Anecdote		

3 Write the section of your speech here.

Extension activity

Can you use all the persuasive features listed in the table?

1.3.8 Chapter reflection

As you come to the end of the unit, you should be able to respond to the inquiry question that has framed your learning: ***How can texts share who we are and what is most important to us?***

1 How has your learning in this unit addressed this inquiry question?

2 What new questions has this unit raised for you?

3 Now, let's turn this inquiry question into a statement to summarise your personal connection to the learning of this unit.

I use texts to share who I am and what is most important to me.

Write down your response to this statement, using these questions as prompts.

Who am I? What is my personal context? What do I value? Who am I as a person?	
What is most important to me? What am I passionate about? What do I think the world needs right now?	

4 How have your reading experiences in this unit shaped your understanding of who you are and what is most important to you? In your response, refer to at least one text read in this unit.

Unit 1: Summative assessment

The summative assessment options below provide opportunities to demonstrate your achievement of the following outcomes and focus areas:

Outcome	EN4-RVL-01 Reading, Viewing and Listening to Texts	EN4-URB-01 Understanding and responding to texts B	EN4-ECA-01 Expressing ideas and composing texts A	EN4-ECB-01 Expressing ideas and composing texts B
Focus Area	Reading, viewing and listening skills	Theme Perspective and Context Argument	Text Features: Persuasive	Planning, Monitoring and Revising

Option 1:

The Conversation Australia is a digital news site that shares opinion articles on current issues. They have asked teens, like you, to write and submit an opinion article about an issue that you feel is important. You must persuade readers that this is also an issue that they should care about.

Be inspired by the texts you have read in this unit to:

- Develop a perspective on an issue of importance aligned with your personal values.
- Establish an argument and build your argument with a logical sequence of ideas.
- Share experiences from your personal context to illustrate your ideas.
- Create and maintain personal voice in your response.
- Use various persuasive language features to influence your audience.

Option 2:

Choose a person that you think should win the next Young Australian of the Year Award and write a persuasive speech from their point of view about an issue they think all Australians should take seriously. The person you choose should be connected in some way to this issue, so you will need to do some research.

Be inspired by the texts you have read in this unit to:

- Develop a perspective on an issue of importance aligned with your personal values.
- Establish an argument and build your argument with a logical sequence of ideas.
- Share experiences from your personal context to illustrate your ideas.
- Create and maintain personal voice in your response.
- Use various persuasive language features to influence your audience.

Option 3:

Choose any response you have written in Unit 1. Refine your response now that you have completed the learning in this unit and rewrite a complete composition.

Annotate your complete composition with notes about how the learning and reading in this unit helped you to create a more refined response.

Be inspired by the texts you have read in this unit to:

- Develop a perspective on an issue of importance aligned with your personal values.
- Establish an argument and build your argument with a logical sequence of ideas.
- Share experiences from your personal context to illustrate your ideas.
- Create and maintain personal voice in your response.
- Use various persuasive language features to influence your audience.

Assessment as Learning: Self-Assessment

Does my response:

- ☐ Identify an issue that I think is important?
- ☐ Present a perspective on this issue (i.e., my own opinion or idea)?
- ☐ Build an argument encouraging the audience to change their opinion or act?
- ☐ Experiment with language and style inspired by texts I've read to create my own personal voice.
- ☐ Use at least three persuasive language features effectively to influence my audience?
- ☐ Inclusive language, emotive language, repetition, anecdote, rhetorical question, metaphor, imperative.

What are two strengths of my response?

____

____

____

What area/s of my response do I need to refine further?

____

____

____

UNIT
02

Word of mouth

Unit inquiry question:
How do spoken texts bring stories and words to life?

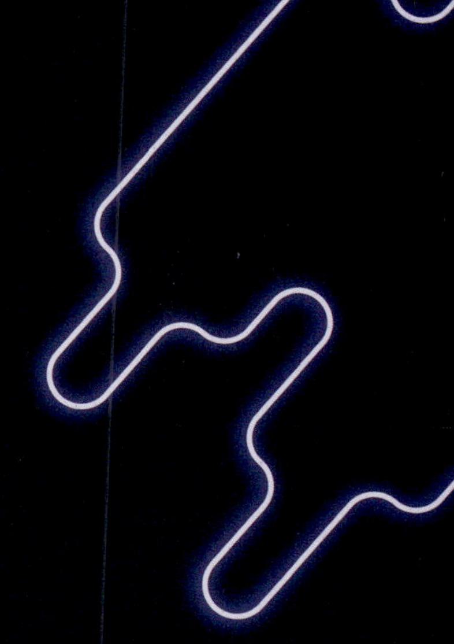

In this unit, students explore oral storytelling, including the role of storytelling in past and present societies and how we are immersed into the world of stories through spoken forms. Students are introduced to drama and performance poetry as two forms of storytelling. They investigate the codes and conventions of these forms to appreciate how they share stories by 'word of mouth'. Students closely examine the styles of one performance poet and one playwright to represent ideas.

To address the focus inquiry question of the unit, students will engage with learning in three chapters:

Chapter 4
The traditions of storytelling

In this chapter, students will reflect on their personal experiences of listening to and sharing stories. They will explore the historical traditions of oral storytelling as well as how we continue to share stories in our modern world. Students will also be introduced to the ways in which stories are a representation of our world and human experience.

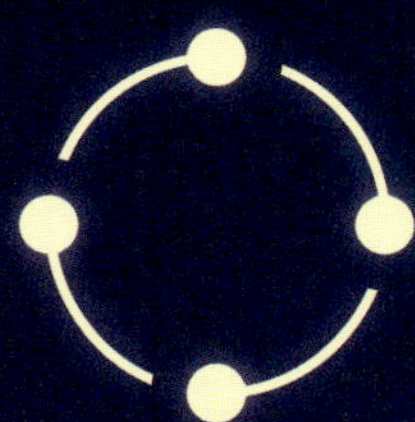

Chapter 5
Giving words a voice

In this chapter, students will explore performance poetry as a form of oral storytelling. They will be introduced to the codes and conventions of this form and closely examine the style of one performance poet to represent ideas and experiences through voice.

Chapter 6
Words on stage

In this final chapter, students will investigate drama as another form of oral storytelling. They will be introduced to the codes and conventions of drama and closely examine the style of one playwright to represent ideas and experiences on stage.

The learning activities within each chapter and the summative assessment options (on page 94) provide opportunities to assess student achievement of the following outcomes:

Outcome and Focus Area	Content point
EN4-RVL-01 Reading, viewing and listening to texts	**Reading, viewing and listening for meaning**
	Explore the main ideas and thematic concerns posed by a text for meaning Engage with the ways texts contain layers of meaning, or multiple meanings Understand how language use evolves over time and in different places and cultures, and is influenced by technological and social developments
EN4-URA-01 Understanding and responding to texts A	**Representation**
	Explore how language and text are acts of representation that range from objective to subjective and may offer layers of literal or implied meanings, and apply this understanding in own texts
	Code and convention
	Use appropriate metalanguage to describe how meaning is constructed through linguistic and stylistic elements in texts Understand how language forms, features and structures, in a variety of texts, vary according to context, purpose and audience, and demonstrate this understanding through written, spoken, visual and multimodal responses
EN4-URB-01 Understanding and responding to texts B	**Style**
	Describe the distinctive rhetorical and aesthetic qualities of a text that contribute to its textual style, and reflect on these qualities in own texts Identify elements of an author's work that represent their distinct style
EN4-ECA-01 Expressing ideas and composing texts A	**Representing**
	Apply codes and conventions of written, spoken, visual and multimodal texts to enhance meaning and create tone, atmosphere and mood
	Speaking
	Communicate information, ideas and viewpoints using verbal and/or nonverbal language, including gestural features, to enhance and clarify meaning Deliver spoken, signed or communicated texts with effective control of intonation, emphasis, volume, pace and timing

Chapter 4

The Traditions of Storytelling

Chapter overview

In this chapter you will reflect on your personal experiences of listening to and sharing stories. You will explore the historical traditions of oral storytelling and how we continue to share stories in our modern age. You will also be introduced to the ways in which stories are a representation of our world and human experience.

Success criteria: In this chapter, I will be successful when I can ...

- describe the traditions of oral storytelling
- explain how storytelling has evolved over time and in different places and cultures, and is influenced by technological and social developments
- explain how various stories represent aspects of our world and human experience
- reflect on personal experiences of listening to and sharing stories.

Chapter inquiry questions

- What are the historical traditions of storytelling?
- How do we continue to share stories in our modern world?
- How are stories a representation of us and our world?

Key vocabulary

- Storytelling
- Traditions
- Evolve
- Representation

What are the historical traditions of storytelling?

PAUSE AND DISCUSS: Before you read about the historical traditions of storytelling, make some predictions by discussing the questions below with a partner.

- How long do you think we have been telling stories for?
- What do you think some of the first stories were about?
- What do you think makes a good storyteller?

It is believed that humans have been sharing stories for as long as we have had language. Although you may think of books as being the main way stories are shared, the earliest form of storytelling, and one that continues today, is the art of **oral storytelling**. Oral storytelling involves sharing stories and experiences with listeners through voice. In our earliest civilisations, this would likely have occurred around a campfire. Even today, when we gather to hear a story, we often sit in a semi-circle with our eyes and ears focused on the storyteller. Listeners participate by engaging with the storyteller, who aims to entertain the audience and may even mould the story to suit the needs of the audience. Storytelling may involve a combination of narrative stories, poetry, music and dance.

2.4.1 Warm-up

Campfire storytime

It's time to tell each other stories by the (fictious) campfire. Gather in a group of five to eight people in a semi-circle.

Each person will take it in turns to tell a one-minute story to the group. The group must select a character, setting and problem combination for the storyteller to use as the basis for their story. Remember, a good storyteller will tell the story with passion, may exaggerate aspects of the story and will know when to pause for effect!

2.4.2 Reading, viewing and listening to texts

We can look at history to help us understand more about the earliest stories ever told. Read and view the following texts to learn more.

The world's oldest story? Astronomers say global myths about 'seven sisters' stars may reach back 100,000 years

By Ray Norris, The Conversation, *22 December 2020*

In the northern sky in December is a beautiful cluster of stars known as the Pleiades, or the 'seven sisters'. Look carefully and you will probably count six stars. So why do we say there are seven of them?

Many cultures around the world refer to the Pleiades as 'seven sisters', and also tell quite similar stories about them. After studying the motion of the stars very closely, we believe these stories may date back 100,000 years to a time when the constellation looked quite different.

In Greek mythology, the Pleiades were the seven daughters of the Titan Atlas. He was forced to hold up the sky for eternity, and was therefore unable to protect his daughters. To save the sisters from the hunter Orion, Zeus transformed them into stars. But the story says one sister fell in love with a mortal and went into hiding, which is why we only see six stars.

A similar story is found among Aboriginal groups across Australia. In many Australian Aboriginal cultures, the Pleiades are a group of young girls, and are often associated with sacred women's ceremonies and stories. The Pleiades are also important as an element of Aboriginal calendars and astronomy, and for several groups their first rising at dawn marks the start of winter. ...

Similar 'lost Pleiad' stories are found in European, African, Asian, Indonesian, Native American and Aboriginal Australian cultures. Many cultures regard the cluster as having seven stars, but acknowledge only six are normally visible, and then have a story to explain why the seventh is invisible.

Scan the QR code to view the full article.

1 According to this article, what is the world's oldest story?

2 Why do you think so many cultures would have been connected by this story?

3 The article says that other cultures across the world have stories about what happened to the seventh sister. Research one of these stories from another culture and write a summary below.

2.4.3 Expressing ideas and composing texts A

What do you think happened to the seventh sister? Write a brief story about the seven sisters and why the seventh is missing from the constellation.

Extension activity

The article refers to Greek mythology, which is a collection of stories and legends about Greek gods and goddesses, heroes and monsters, rituals and traditions.

Research one of the Greek myths listed below and create a comic strip that reflects the myth:

- The Story of Chaos
- The Clash of the Titans
- Pandora's Box
- Theseus and the Minotaur

2.4.4 Reading, viewing and listening to texts

Australian storytelling

We know that Aboriginal and Torres Strait Islander cultures are among the oldest living cultures on Earth. The term 'Dreamtime' refers to stories about how the world, universe and humans came into existence, and there is evidence that the stories date back over 65,000 years. Dreamtime stories were told orally and through art.

Use the QR code to access the ABC Dust Echoes website, which contains twelve animated Dreamtime stories from Central Arnhem Land. After looking at the stories, see if you can predict what part of creation each one may reflect.

Examine the list of Dreamtime stories on the Dust Echoes website.

1. Make a group of four students.
2. Allocate one Dreamtime story to each person in the group.
3. All students with the same Dreamtime story in the class, come together to discuss the story. Use the questions on the Dust Echoes website to guide your discussion.
4. Return to your original group.
5. Share the Dreamtime story you discussed with the remaining members of your group.

Individually, complete the activity below.

1. Which of the Dreamtime stories did you enjoy the most? Why?

____

____

2. Why do you think these Dreamtime stories have survived for so long?

____

____

____

Extension activity

Earliest written story

Many sources suggest that the 'Epic of Gilgamesh' is the earliest surviving written story. The epic tale was written on clay tablets nearly 4,000 ago in ancient Mesopotamia (modern day Iraq). The story tells the tale of Gilgamesh, the king of the city of Uruk, who goes on a quest to find immortality.

Research and read about the story online. With a partner, discuss whether you think this story is relevant for us today and what this suggests about what we value in modern life.

2.4.5 Reading, viewing and listening to texts

Storytelling through song

Song has long been used as a form of oral storytelling, sharing cultural traditions and experiences. In our modern world, songs continue to connect people all over the world. Songs are also a powerful way to comment on important issues in society. Here is an extract from the song 'From Little Things Big Things Grow' (1991) by Australian songwriters Paul Kelly and Kev Carmody. The song tells the story of the Gurindji Strike (Wave Hill walk-off) as an important part of the struggle for land rights and reconciliation for Aboriginal and Torres Strait Islander peoples.

From Little Things Big Things Grow

by Paul Kelly and Kev Carmody

Gather 'round people, I'll tell you a story
An eight-year long story of power and pride
British Lord Vestey and Vincent Lingiari
Were opposite men on opposite sides ...

From little things big things grow
From little things big things grow

Gurindji were working for nothing but rations
Where once they had gathered the wealth of the land
Daily the oppression got tighter and tighter
Gurindji decided they must make a stand

They picked up their swags and started off walking
At Wattie Creek they sat themselves down
Now it don't sound like much but it sure got tongues talking
Back at the homestead and then in the town

From little things big things grow
From little things big things grow

Vestey man said, 'I'll double your wages
8 quid a week you'll have in your hand'
Vincent said, 'Uh-uh we're not talking about wages
We're sitting right here 'til we get our land'

1 What does the song tell you about the Gurindji Strike?

2 The chorus is the simple repetition of the phrase: 'From little things big things grow'. What do you think this phrase means within the context of this story?

3 What role do you think this song plays in sharing this important story?

2.4.6 Expressing ideas and composing texts A

Now that you have read about some of the early traditions of storytelling, think about some of the stories from your early life. Perhaps it's the story of your birth, the story of your family's origins, a fun holiday you had as a child, the day you lost your first tooth or a make-believe adventure you had with a friend. It's your turn to become a storyteller.
Share one story from your early life. You could choose to share this story as:

- a series of pictures, inspired by the Dust Echoes Dreamtime stories
- a narrative story, inspired by Greek mythology or the Epic of Gilgamesh
- song lyrics, inspired by Paul Kelly and Kev Carmody.

Gather in a small group to share your story.

How do we continue to share stories in our modern world?

While we may no longer sit around a campfire at night and tell tales, we continue to share stories. Advances in technology have meant that the way we share stories has evolved. In our modern world, we use the internet, especially social media, to share our experiences and our story with the world. In fact, a popular Instagram feature is even called 'Stories'. Social media allows stories to be shared via voice, text, video, animation, music, dance or body language, among other things.

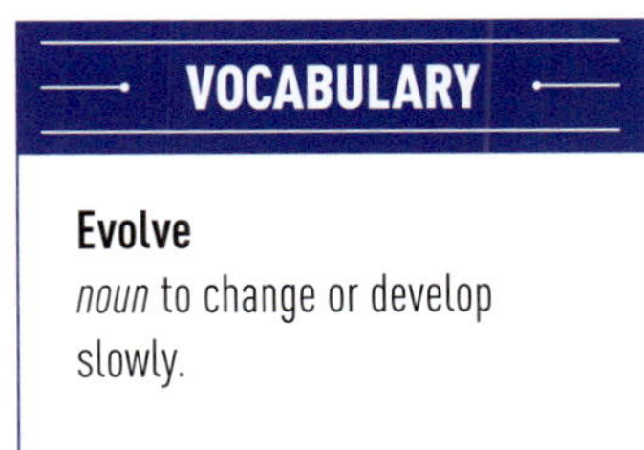

2.4.7 Reading, viewing and listening to texts

Online storytelling behaviour

Social media allows you to have control of your story. You become a storyteller every time you post, like or share online. But how do you know that the story that you see is real? And does it really matter if it isn't?

Use the QR code to watch the video 'Legal consequences of online behaviour'.

1 The video tells us that stories can be shared instantly via social media. Explain one advantage and one disadvantage of using social media as a form of instant storytelling.

____

____

____

2 How can you tell if the story you are seeing online is real, fake or just a rumour?

____

____

____

3 How have laws been created to respond to negative behaviours online?

____

____

____

2.4.8 Reading, viewing and listening to texts

Social storytelling

A 'trend' is something that spreads quickly and appeals to a wide range of audiences. You may have seen dance trends or music trends on various social media platforms. A trend is a form of modern storytelling. The following article extract from *The Conversation* discusses the concept of 'social storytelling' with music.

Encanto, TikTok and the art of social storytelling: why music is not just for listening anymore

By Kai Riemer and Sandra Peter, The Conversation, *23 March 2022*

We need to talk about Bruno. The theme song from Disney's hit movie *Encanto* ('We don't talk about Bruno') has become the first song from an animated movie to top the US charts for multiple weeks. How did this come about? The answer is, once again, TikTok.

At the heart of the phenomenon are viral challenges or trends, in which creators use short clips from a song that are re-used by thousands or millions of other users in their videos. ...

Tom van Laer, Associate Professor of Narratology at The University of Sydney Business School, explains what makes for good storytelling: 'For a good story, you need three things. A story has a plot and a character ... That's the minimum for a story. For a good story you need a third thing, which is a dramatic curve.'

And this is where the music comes into play. When a challenge or trend emerges on TikTok, it always features the same clip from a particular song, which serves as a common story element across all those videos. ...

Because the clip is instantly recognisable by the audience it ties together all the videos that make up a TikTok challenge or trend.

1 What does the article suggest about how social media and music are used as forms of storytelling?

____

____

____

2 Music was also used as one of the earliest forms of storytelling. Have we really changed that much in how we share stories? Refer to the ideas from this article in your response.

____

____

____

How are stories a representation of us and our world?

The stories we tell and the ones that we have been telling for centuries are all a **representation** of how we see the world and our human experience.

What is representation?

A representation is the way that a storyteller depicts things or ideas, or the view that they have about a particular idea. Storytellers are always influenced by their experiences, beliefs, values, cultural background and the audience of the text they are creating. The storyteller makes deliberate decisions in their text to represent an idea in a certain way.

For example, a writer who has grown up swimming and living by the beach may represent the ocean as peaceful and calm. However, another writer who had a previously bad experience in the ocean may represent it as a dangerous and unpredictable force of nature.

2.4.9 Reading, viewing and listening to texts

Stories as representation

The stories you tell the world are a representation of the way you see aspects of the world. In a similar way, most stories represent common aspects of our human experience, our shared desires and flaws. Some stories represent positive and idyllic ways of living, while others represent cautionary tales to warn us about consequences of our actions. All storytellers make a conscious or deliberate choice about how they represent the world in their text.

1 What representation does this social media user aim to reflect in this post?

2 Explain how the post uses text and visuals to create this representation.

2.4.10 Understanding and responding to texts A

For each text listed that you have examined in this chapter, identify what the storyteller represents about each topic.

Text	Topic	What does this text represent about this topic?
Dust Echoes	Creation and the land	
From Little Things Big Things Grow	Land rights	
Legal consequences of online behaviour	Online behaviour	

2.4.11 Chapter reflection

1 What have you learned about the oral traditions of storytelling?

2 What have you learned about how storytelling has evolved over time?

____

____

____

3 What have you learned about why humans like storytelling?

____

____

____

4 'Stories are wild creatures', the monster said. 'When you let them loose, who knows what havoc they might wreak?' – Patrick Ness, *A Monster Calls*

a What power do stories have if we share them with others?

____

____

b Create another analogy (comparison) to reflect the power of spoken stories.

Stories are like ____,

when they are told they ____

____

5 Reflect on a story you have read or heard lately. What representation of the world does this story provide?

____

____

____

____

____

____

____

____

Chapter 5

GIVING WORDS A VOICE

Chapter overview

In this chapter, you will examine how poetry is a form of storytelling. You will look closely at the style of performance poetry and be introduced to its codes and conventions as well as some poets. Finally, you will examine the style of the performance poet Solli Raphael and the way he uses his poetry as a representation of his ideas and feelings.

Success criteria: In this chapter, I will be successful when I can ...

- identify the codes and conventions of performance poetry
- describe the poetic style of performance poets
- explain how performance poets use codes and conventions to represent ideas and engage audiences with stories
- reflect on personal experiences of viewing performance poetry
- create and perform poetry that represents my ideas and feelings.

Chapter inquiry questions

- How is poetry a form of storytelling?
- What are the codes and conventions of performance poetry?
- How can I be inspired by the style of one performance poet to give my words a voice?

Key vocabulary

- Performance poetry
- Codes and conventions
- Representation
- Style

How is poetry a form of storytelling?

Poetry has been used to tell stories and share experiences for many centuries. In earlier times when people could not read, poetry was used to share not only stories but news and messages. While there are many different styles of poetry, there are a few things that most poems have in common. Poetry is often ...

- very emotive, which means that the poet usually aims to trigger certain emotions for the audience
- crafted with descriptions or comparisons to create mental images for the audience to connect with their emotions
- intended to be read aloud, so there will be quite a lot of sounds written into poetry.

Poetry is also another form of **representation**. Poets use their poems to represent their feelings and views on the world. Here, Pádraig Ó Tuama explains why people write poetry:

'... deeper than the craft of poetry is the why of poetry. Why did the poet write this? Or, perhaps, why did the poet need to write this? The poet needed to make a record. It's evidence of their existence; like our ancestors' handprints on the wall of a cave, an "I am here".'

This suggests that poetry is a representation of the thoughts and feelings of a poet at a particular time in the world's history. Poets are storytellers of their generation, helping audiences understand each other's experiences and stories.

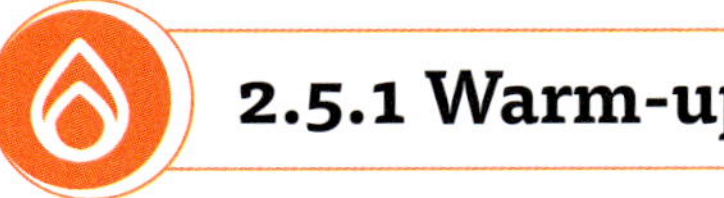

What is poetry?

Make a list of three things you have always been told about poetry or things you already know about it.

- ____________________
- ____________________
- ____________________

Now, read this description of poetry.

'A poem is a difficult thing to define. What is it? It's a little block of ink on a page, sometimes five lines long, sometimes fifty. It's a house of memory. It's a clockwork thing you can carry in your pocket; take it out, set it to go, and it goes. Tick-tock-tick-tock, it says, sometimes rhyming with itself. Some poems are full of love, and some of anger; some poems remember things that shouldn't be forgotten, other poems fantasise about the future, acting as a warning for today. Some sound like a song, others like a story.'

- Pádraig Ó Tuama – Poetry Unbound: 50 Poems to Open Your World

What other ideas does this description give you about poetry?

Narrative poetry

Narrative poetry is a style of poetry that tells a story using traditional narrative elements like plot, setting and characters. Usually, a narrative poem is quite long. **Ballads** and **verse novels** are two styles of narrative poetry that you will now examine.

What is a ballad?

A ballad is a style of narrative poetry that aims to tell a story. Traditionally, ballads were sung or set to music, another way of sharing stories orally. Ballads usually have a consistent **rhyme scheme** and may sometimes repeat lines to form a chorus.

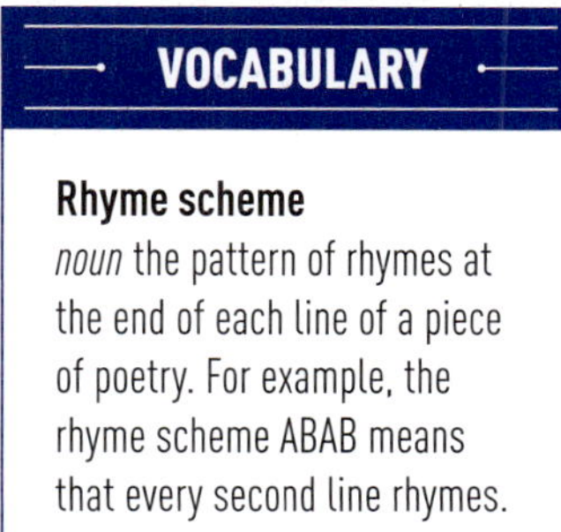

VOCABULARY

Rhyme scheme
noun the pattern of rhymes at the end of each line of a piece of poetry. For example, the rhyme scheme ABAB means that every second line rhymes.

2.5.2 Reading, viewing and listening to texts

Bush poet Banjo Patterson was a well-known Australian storyteller. Here is an extract from one of his ballad poems 'Mulga Bill's Bicycle' (1896). This story is best heard aloud – in small groups, take turns reading the stanzas of the poem aloud. Use the punctuation to guide your delivery of the poem.

Mulga Bill's Bicycle

'Twas Mulga Bill, from Eaglehawk, that caught the cycling craze;
He turned away the good old horse that served him many days;
He dressed himself in cycling clothes, resplendent to be seen;
He hurried off to town and bought a shining new machine;
And as he wheeled it through the door, with air of lordly pride,
The grinning shop assistant said, 'Excuse me, can you ride?'

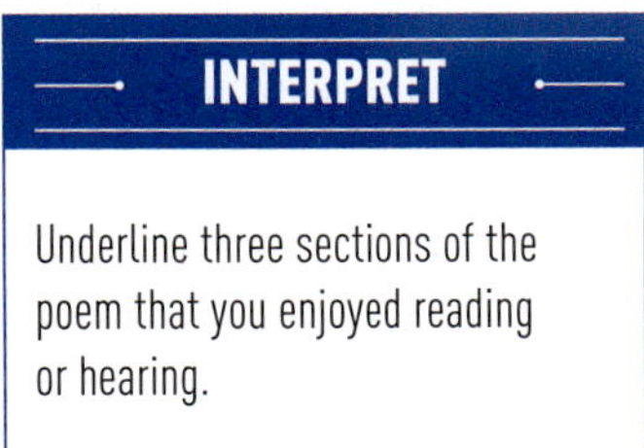

INTERPRET

Underline three sections of the poem that you enjoyed reading or hearing.

'See here, young man,' said Mulga Bill, 'from Walgett to the sea,
From Conroy's Gap to Castlereagh, there's none can ride like me.
I'm good all round at everything, as everybody knows,
Although I'm not the one to talk – I hate a man that blows.
But riding is my special gift, my chiefest, sole delight;
Just ask a wild duck can it swim, a wildcat can it fight.' ...

'Twas Mulga Bill, from Eaglehawk, that sought his own abode,
That perched above the Dead Man's Creek, beside the mountain road.
He turned the cycle down the hill and mounted for the fray,
But ere he'd gone a dozen yards it bolted clean away.
It left the track, and through the trees, just like a silver streak,
It whistled down the awful slope towards the Dead Man's Creek.

It shaved a stump by half an inch, it dodged a big white-box:
The very wallaroos in fright went scrambling up the rocks,
The wombats hiding in their caves dug deeper underground,
As Mulga Bill, as white as chalk, sat tight to every bound.
It struck a stone and gave a spring that cleared a fallen tree,
It raced beside a precipice as close as close could be;
And then as Mulga Bill let out one last despairing shriek
It made a leap of twenty feet into the Dead Man's Creek.

STRUCTURE

Label the rhyme scheme of the poem.

1 Write a few words next to each section of the poem to describe what happens to Mulga Bill.

2 What do you think this ballad aims to teach us?

3 One reason why this ballad is engaging is the use of rhyme. Why do you think the rhyme kept you engaged in this story?

4 Another reason this ballad is so entertaining is because there are some exaggerated descriptions. Find an example of exaggeration in the story and explain why this would entertain listeners.

What is a verse novel?

Another style of narrative poetry, a **verse novel** tells a novel-long story through a series of poems. This style of narrative is popular because it experiments with structure, it can sometimes capture the point of view of many characters and some audiences find it easier to read a complete story in this way.

2.5.3 Understanding and responding to texts A

Here is an extract from the verse novel *Bindi* by Kirli Saunders (2020), written from the point of view of 11-year-old Bindi who narrates her experience of a bushfire in her town.

Maths Class

By Kirli Saunders

A heavy grey looms over the footy field today
and we hide away inside.

In class, we make lists in *descending* order.

I watch ash fall from the sky

and dream the karat,
that we danced for,

will *add*,
and *multiply*,

subtracting the canbe.

As the class maps maths solutions,

I think of one for our
climate crisis.

I know Old People
have the answer.

VOCABULARY

Karat
noun karat is the Gundungurra word for rain, pronounced like 'carrot'.

VOCABULARY

Canbe
noun canbe is the Gundungurra word for fire, pronounced like 'can bee'.

LANGUAGE

Circle any mathematical words used throughout the poem.

1 What does this poem show that Bindi is worried about?

2 Why are mathematical words used in this poem?

3 What **representation** does the writer use this poem to reflect about the environment and climate?

What are the codes and conventions of performance poetry?

Performance poetry is sometimes called slam poetry or spoken word poetry. It is a style of poetry written specifically to be performed aloud to an audience rather than printed; its beats and rhythm have a lot in common with hip hop and beat poetry.

Australian Poetry Slam Champion Solli Raphael explains what performance poetry means to him:

'Slam poetry, spoken word poetry and rap are all different, but what makes these art forms so special is that you use a stack of emotion to express your thoughts to the audience. For me, being able to put words together to create something exceptional that inspires the crowd is the true meaning of slam poetry. I love writing about my feelings and beliefs, mixing in creative ideas and keeping to a certain structure, rhythm or beat.'

2.5.4 Viewing and listening reflection

To become familiar with the style of performance poetry, access and view Omar Musa's performance of his poem 'Play On'.

Play On

By Omar Musa

This is a warning to everyone.

Tomorrow is not your friend.

Tomorrow is a visitor whose arrival you cannot prepare for, whose mood swings you cannot anticipate. You cannot anticipate because you never know whether he arrives at your door bearing flowers or a handgun, but you know that he approaches by the hour.

This is a warning.

Never let the fire in the lamp burn low. Never stop making your music, even if the record is scratched, the needle is snapped and the mic is unplugged – play on.

Even when you stand looking out over treacherous reefs, where coral is like the blades of razors, where the sky is glimmering coal above sharks and shimmering shoals. Where you wade through tides of information (some right, some wrong, some plain insane) waves of opinion so powerful they threaten to drown you – play on.

Even when it feels as if friendship is a battleground, where the breeze is rich with ego and mistrust, where the blazing sun is blackened by a billion arrows that sing with the clarity of birds. Where we exchange pugilistic words in bourbon bars and hotted up cars, where we feel as if we are the flotsam and jetsam of marooned ideals – play on.

Even when the rejection letters stack up like a pyramid and they tell you that you have no flow and that no-one wants to hear an Aussie rapper and no radio station will play you and you scream and scream and nobody hears you – play on.

But I'm not sure why we should, when clearly the odds are stacked against us. And I know that men's hearts are pastures that bloom with darkness.

All I know is that I am lucky to be here and that some day soon this man of passion and lust will be ashes and dust. And they will sprinkle me back into the soil from which I sprang and I don't want my final whisper to be a lament. I want to say that I leapt from the cliffs when the moment demanded it. That I sipped from the chalice when it was handed to me. That even though the record was scratched, the needle was snapped and the mic was unplugged, I played on.

This is a warning to everyone. Tomorrow is not your friend. So never let the fire in the lamp burn low. Cause you never know when today might end.

1 Journal your thoughts in your notebook, after viewing this video. What did you enjoy about Musa's poetry performance?

Codes and conventions

Codes and conventions are the arrangement of language features and structures specific to a form of text that help create meaning. The codes and conventions help you recognise and create familiarity with the type of text you are reading. For example, when you read a novel, you expect it to contain sentences and paragraphs, description and dialogue plus plot, setting and characters, just to name a few.

Performance poetry uses many codes and conventions you would associate with traditional poetry. However, there are other codes and conventions used specifically for the oral nature of this style of poetry.

Structural freedom

Performance poetry is often written in **free verse**, which means that the poems don't follow one set structure, but rather follow natural patterns of speech, like a conversation. Despite this freedom, there are still some technical codes and conventions that may apply. Performance poems are made up of **lines**. These lines may be put together into **stanzas**, which may look like a paragraph. Some performance poems include punctuation to signal how the poem should be read or listened to.

Choose two lines from Musa's poem 'Play On'. Write the lines below and punctuate with **commas** to show brief pauses or connected ideas and **full stops** to show where longer pauses are required.

____

____

Slang

Many performance poets have their own unique style or draw on their specific culture and background for the language they use in their work. **Slang** or colloquial expression is the use of informal language specific to a group of people. This type of language helps performance poets create their unique voice and relate to their audience.

Make a list of slang words and phrases used by a specific group or culture that you or somebody that you know belongs to. Alternatively, think about a specific group or culture that you have seen on the internet or on TV.

- Group: ______________________________________
- Slang words: __________________________________

  ____

Rhythm and beat

Rhythm is the regular pattern of sounds in a text. Performance poetry does not need to rhyme to create rhythm, nor does it need to follow strict rules. Instead, poets may create a **beat** using language, like repeating phrases or stressing certain syllables. When performing the poem, the speaker may also alternate pace (speed), pause and volume to control the rhythm and beat.

Find a section of Musa's poem 'Play On' that you think has rhythm. Write that section below.

____

____

1 What choices has Musa made to create rhythm in this section?

____

____

2 How does the rhythm in this section help to convey Musa's message?

____

____

Figurative language

In Unit 1 you learned about how language can be used figuratively to reflect ideas, emotions or thoughts. Generally, figurative language refers to things in a non-literal way, so requires some interpretation.

Similes and **metaphors** (which you learned about in Unit 1) are examples of figurative language that are often used by performance poets to represent ideas and engage audiences. **Idioms** – phrases that aren't meant to be taken literally – are common in poetry. For example, someone may say that it's 'raining cats and dogs' when there is a large amount of rain, or that 'time flies when you're having fun'. Another form of figurative language is **personification**, where a poet gives human qualities to non-human items. For example, the trees might dance in the wind, or the stars might wink in the night sky.

These forms of figurative language are used commonly by performance poets as they aim to help audiences create a mental image and connect emotionally to their words.

Interpret each of these figurative phrases from Musa's poem 'Play On'. What does he really mean?

- 'Tomorrow is a visitor whose arrival you cannot prepare for':

  ____

- 'Never let the fire in the lamp burn low':

____

- 'Waves of opinion so powerful':

____

- 'Friendship is a battleground':

____

- 'Odds are stacked against us':

____

Direct address

Remember, this style of poetry is created to be performed to an audience, so engagement with listeners is a key part of the style. Some performance poetry may also directly address the audience, asking the audience to take action or change their thoughts and opinions on a topic.

1 Find an example of direct address in Musa's poem.

____

2 What overall action does Musa want from his audience? How do you know?

____

____

How can I be inspired by the style of one performance poet to give my words a voice?

As you have learned, performance poetry provides lots of freedom for poets to create their own unique style. **Style** refers to the characteristic ways the poet chooses to express their ideas. Performance poets will make decisions about the language, structure, rhythm and ideas of their poetry and over time will develop a style that makes their work recognisable. You will also develop your own style as a poet.

2.5.5 Understanding and responding to texts A

CONTEXT

'When I started writing the poem 'Game Changer', I had it in my mind that it was going to be about me. I don't mean that in a selfish way, but I wanted to influence how people live by offering ideas on an environmentally friendly lifestyle and encouraging them to help others within their community. But as I wrote the poem, I felt it was more a representation of my generation. Many of us, like you and me, are trying our hardest to make changes to help our future be better.'

Source: Solli Raphael

In this part of the chapter, you will closely examine the style of Solli Raphael, who at the age of 12 became the youngest winner of the Australian Poetry Slam competition. Start by reading his poem 'Game Changer'.

Game Changer

By Solli Raphael

I am a gamechanger.
I am a game change, change game, low age, no rage,
onstage arranger.
I am both yes and no, stay and go, catch and throw,
goodbye and hello, forest ranger.
I am the lightning that makes the thunder – rumble.
I am the space – outside of the box.
I am the magnetic field between the moon and the sea.
I am the quality – in equality.
I am the undiscovered myth in wordsmith.
I am the reality, of my own big dreams.
I am the curve of the world, that I can only just see.
I am a gamechanger.
I am a curly hair very rare level of sublimity.
I am a square of fresh air.
I am the fair in share, a spare pair of prayers for stairs
to infinity.
I am a gamechanger.
And no matter how much **you** change,
No matter how much the **world** changes,
No matter how much **change changes.**
I will always be changing, as, I, am a gamechanger.

LANGUAGE

Anaphora is the repetition of words at the beginning of a sentence or phrase. Underline examples of anaphora in this poem.

LANGUAGE

Circle each repetition of the word 'change'. How many times does the word appear in the poem?

1 What is Raphael's message about change in this poem?

____

____

2 Raphael uses a series of metaphors to represent himself. Select one metaphor and explain what he is using to show about himself.

3 How do you think this poem should be performed? Label the poem above with your ideas, considering pace, pause, volume, stressing of syllables, beat and rhythm.

2.5.6 Viewing and listening reflection

Next, access and view Raphael's performance of the poem 'Game Changer' via the QR code.

Journal your thoughts on viewing and listening to Raphael's performance of this poem. Did the performance of the poem match how you thought the poem should be performed? How did his delivery of the poem, including the creation of rhythm, enhance its message?

Now read this extract of 'Australian Air', another of Raphael's performance poems.

Australian Air

By Solli Raphael

Since the day of our arrival, we've been killing our own
survival, and it's vital, that our sidle title is put aside, so
we can become ONE with our rivals.

We breathe in, we breathe out.

So don't sit around waiting for your life to caper, instead –
grab your pens and your paper – your voices and your eyes,
so we can reach for the sky, and look down on the world,
and tell them why,
we need to make a change

To our lives.

Because we don't have to be these average everyday
humans anymore.

We can show this world what we feel, see and think,

and that might be the hidden link,
between peace, war and humans causing our own race to
be extinct.

And sometimes

We need to breathe out,

just so we can breathe in kindness

and passion.

Scan the QR code to view Raphael's performance of the complete poem 'Australian Air'.

2.5.7 Understanding and responding to texts B

1 Now that you have examined two of Raphael's poems, describe how he uses these codes and conventions of performance poetry to create his own style.

Code or convention	Describe Raphael's use of this code or convention	Example from one of the poems
Slang or informal language		
Figurative language		
Rhythm		
Direct address		

2 Imagine you have been asked to introduce Raphael at a Poetry Slam competition. Write a brief description of his style as a performance poet as part of this introduction.

2.5.8 Expressing ideas and composing texts A

Inspired by the style of Solli Raphael and the other poetic storytellers you have read about in this chapter, create your own poem that represents your thoughts and feelings on an idea or topic. You may be asked to share your poem aloud with a small group.

PAUSE: First, you must plan your composition.

Topic:

Intended message:

Ideas to support message:

Style of poem (circle one): narrative poem / performance poem

Other codes and conventions:

Write your poem here:

2.5.9 Chapter reflection

1 What have you learned about how poetry gives stories and words a voice?

____

____

____

2 Reflect on one poem you read in this chapter. Why did this poem engage you?

____

____

____

3 What you have you learned about your own developing style as a poet?

____

____

____

4 Let's return to the unit inquiry question: ***How do spoken texts bring stories and words to life?*** How have your reading experiences in this chapter addressed the inquiry question?

____

____

____

Chapter 6
WORDS ON STAGE

Chapter overview

In this chapter, you will investigate drama as another form of oral storytelling. You will be introduced to the codes and conventions of drama scripts and closely examine the style of one playwright to represent ideas and experiences on stage. Your reading and viewing of drama in this chapter will inspire you to construct your own drama script to represent your understanding of its codes and conventions.

Success criteria: In this chapter, I will be successful when I can ...

- identify the codes and conventions of drama
- describe the dramatic style of playwrights
- explain how drama scripts use codes and conventions to represent ideas and engage audiences with stories
- reflect on my experience of reading and viewing drama
- create a script that represents my ideas and feelings.

Chapter inquiry questions

- How is drama a form of storytelling?
- What are the codes and conventions of drama?
- How can I be inspired by the style of one playwright to give words a stage?

Key vocabulary

- Drama
- Playwright
- Script
- Codes and conventions
- Style

How is drama a form of storytelling?

Drama, acting or performance is one of the oldest forms of storytelling. If you think about it, drama is simply the acting out of different scenarios or experiences. While you may be more familiar with acting in movies or on television, the performance of drama in theatre is also still a popular form of entertainment. It is believed that drama began when early humans would re-enact events and experiences for others, to share tales, pass down history or entertain. Drama really is sharing stories by word of mouth!

2.6.1 Warm-up

Setting the scene

Read the description of the setting for *Boy Overboard: The Play*, adapted by Patricia Cornelius. Imagine you are seated in the audience of the theatre for this performance.

Setting

A series of platforms at different heights, some suspended, some roped off, create various spaces for the action. One platform is the family house, one a shop, one a block of seating at a stadium; one is the back of a truck littered in sacks under which the family hide. One serves as the docks, one the deck of a boat. They can be moved in and out and around the performance space to accommodate the action. The platforms are like rafts – isolated, floating and vulnerable. There is a boot of a car which is either attached to a car or not. There is also an expanse of tents.

1 Make a list of the sights and sounds you might see on the stage in front of you.

____

____

2 On a separate piece of paper, draw how the stage might be set up for this performance.

Drama

Drama as we know it, on a stage in a theatre, originated in Ancient Greece. Stories of the gods were acted out for audiences during festivals, for both entertainment and to celebrate the gods. Western drama evolved further in Rome and, later, during the Middle Ages in Europe.

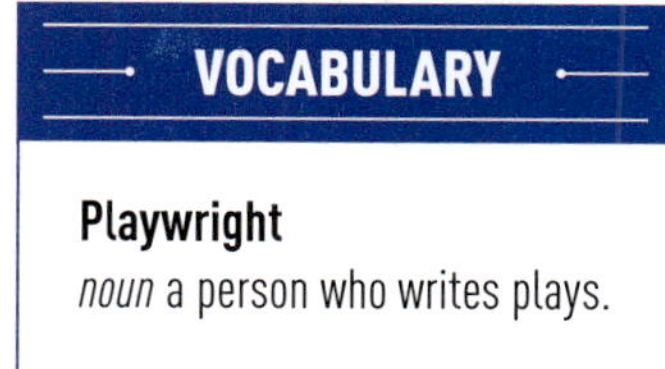

One of the most famous **playwrights** in the world is William Shakespeare (1564–1616), who wrote *Romeo and Juliet*, *Hamlet*, *Macbeth* and *A Midsummer Night's Dream*, to name just a few.

Drama is created for performance. A **drama script** is the story that has been written by the playwright for the actors to perform. In this chapter, you will learn about the codes and conventions of a drama script. However, it is important to always remember that drama is written for a live audience, so not only are stories told through voice but also through body language and action. This means that all your senses are engaged as a member of the audience.

What stories are told in drama?

You will now examine three **styles** of classic drama: tragedy, comedy and musical. Regardless of style, drama aims to tell stories about human experiences and human nature. Drama shows audiences how people may respond to different situations. The stories told through drama also show our similarities and differences as humans.

Tragedy: stories that warn

A **tragedy** often tells stories about serious topics. In this style of play, the audience may see a main character make terrible decisions that ultimately lead to their downfall. A tragedy usually ends with death and destruction, providing audiences with a warning about our human flaws.

Romeo and Juliet by William Shakespeare is an example of a tragedy. Read part of the play's **prologue** (a speech given to the audience at the beginning of the play). Discuss how the underlined sections of the prologue demonstrate elements of the style of tragedy.

Two households, both alike in dignity,
In fair Verona, where we lay our scene,
From ancient grudge break to new mutiny,
Where civil blood makes civil hands unclean.
From forth the fatal loins of these two foes
A pair of star-crossed lovers take their life;
Whose misadventured piteous overthrows
Doth with their death bury their parents' strife.

Comedy: stories that entertain

A **comedy** aims to entertain or amuse the audience. Often the source of this entertainment is a misunderstanding that leads to funny situations. Farce comedies include exaggeration and physical humour, such as slapstick. Comedies tell light-hearted stories that usually show a character overcoming challenges in a humorous way. A comedy may draw the audience's attention to serious issues by making fun of these topics.

Musical: stories with song and dance

Stories are told in **musical** drama through both dialogue (talking) and song. One form of musical is opera, in which orchestral music, singing and dance are used to tell the events of the story and mirror character feelings. A modern, popular style today is musical theatre, which also uses dialogue, song and dance to tell stories, often exaggerating emotions and experiences. These productions are often simply known as musicals.

1 Research the Australian tour of one of the following musicals: *Wicked*, *Cinderella* or *Mary Poppins*. Watch some scenes from the musical production.

2 Describe the style of this production.

____

____

Modern drama: stories of real people

These types of classic drama have evolved into a style now known as **modern drama**. This style continues to share experiences common to humans and tell stories that reflect who we are.

Modern drama is a general term for the way drama and theatre evolved in the early 20th century. Modern drama focuses on everyday real people with everyday real problems. This means that characters will look and talk more like us. The style is focused more on representing ideas than including lots of action. The settings of these plays are also normal, everyday places you would be familiar with.

1 Read the opening to *Two Weeks with the Queen: The Play* adapted by Mary Morris.

Act 1, Scene 1

The music of God Save the Queen *is heard, followed by the plummy voice of Her Majesty delivering her Christmas message. At the Mudford's place MUM and DAD, barefoot and dressed in shorts, singlets and paper hats, are fanning themselves with a bit torn off a beer carton. They are watching the Queen's Christmas message on TV. COLIN, also in shorts and very scuffed brown elastic-sided boots, sits some way from them glaring at an open shoe box containing a pair of sensible black school shoes. His kid brother LUKE runs in and out strafing everybody and everything with his new MiG fighter plane. COLIN picks up a shoe and looks at it with distaste.*

Queen And a very merry Christmas to you all.
Colin Merry flamin' Christmas. *[LUKE strafes him.]* Gerroff!
Luke Wanno go?

LUKE does a circle of the room shooting down the enemy and swoops on COLIN again. COLIN throws a shoe at him.

Luke He hit me! Dad, he hit me!
Dad Don't hit your brother Colin.
Colin I didn't ...
Mum You heard your father.
Colin It was him, he started ...
Dad That's enough! We're trying to listen to the Queen here.
Colin Nobody ever listens to me.
Luke That's cos you're not the Queen.
Dad Just keep it down to a roar, eh?

2 What is included in this opening to make the play feel 'real' or to represent the everyday person?

____

____

3 What ideas do you think this play might reflect?

____

____

2.6.2 Expressing ideas and composing texts A

Choose one style of drama you have learned about in this chapter and write the premise for a production in this style. A premise is a summary of the story you wish to tell, including setting, characters and the main problem or issue of the story. Your premise should show an understanding of the style you have chosen.

Use one of the following prompts as inspiration, if needed.

- A family moves into an old castle.
- Long-lost twins find each other.
- A science experiment goes wrong.
- An ordinary night at home become extraordinary.

Write your premise here:

____

____

____

____

____

What are the codes and conventions of drama?

You will now learn about the **codes and conventions** of drama, specifically a drama script written for performance.

A drama narrative written for stage is often known as a play. Like any narrative, a play tells a story through settings, characters and plot. Codes and conventions of plays include: acts and scenes, stage directions, and dialogue, soliloquies, monologues and asides.

> **VOCABULARY**
>
> **Codes and conventions**
> Codes and conventions are the arrangement of language features and structures specific to a form of text that help create meaning. The codes and conventions help you recognise and create familiarity with the type of text you are reading.

Acts and scenes

Plays can be divided into acts and scenes.

Acts group the play into broad sections. Many plays are written with a three-act structure – they have an exposition, a climax and a resolution. The Shakespeare play *A Midsummer Night's Dream* is divided into five acts:

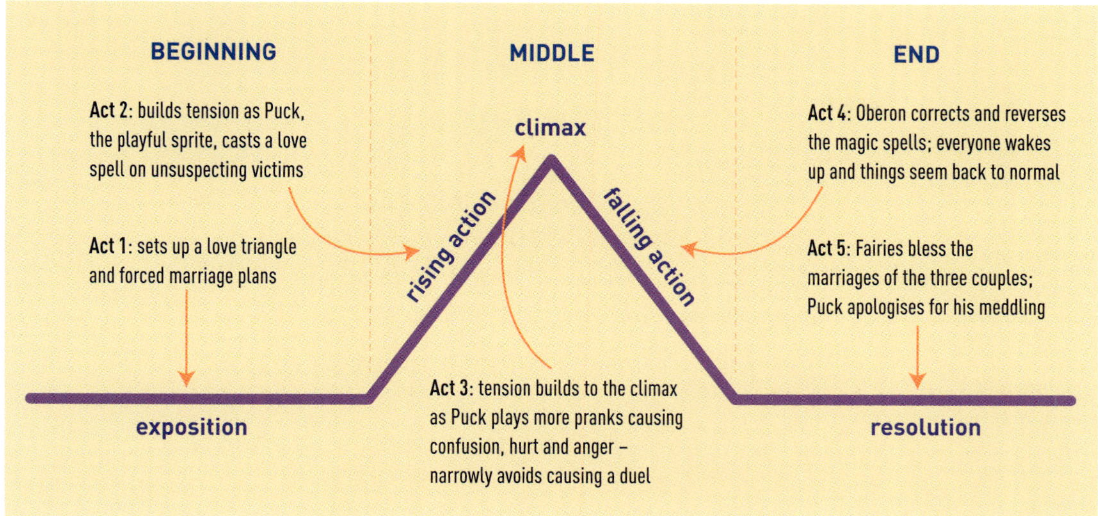

Scenes are then structured within each act to further the story. Scenes can vary in length, depending on what the playwright aims to reveal at that point of the narrative.

Stage directions

Stage directions are usually written in italics and provide important instructions to everyone involved in the play. They provide two kinds of information:

- details of the set, lighting, sound and props (e.g. *A flourish of trumpets*)
- details of the appearance and performance of characters (e.g. *The company returns, two of them dance, then exeunt* – exeunt means they exit).

Dialogue, soliloquies, monologues and asides

Plays are designed to be watched and listened to, not to be read. Characters can deliver their lines in different ways, depending on what will best inform the audience.

Type of speech	Definition
Dialogue	Anything said by one character to another character. Many plays are written mostly in dialogue.
Soliloquy	A speech made by a character when they are alone onstage – it lets the audience know what the character is feeling, but the other characters aren't present or don't hear it.
Monologue	An extended solo speech that other characters can hear.
Aside	Lines spoken by the character directly to the audience – it is understood that other characters present cannot hear them.

Read the extract from the play *A Ghost in My Suitcase*, adapted by Vanessa Bates, and take note of the labelled codes and conventions.

The play tells the story of twelve-year-old Celeste who travels to China to scatter her mother's ashes. She learns that her grandmother, Por Por, is a ghost-hunter, and in this scene she accompanies her to look for ghosts.

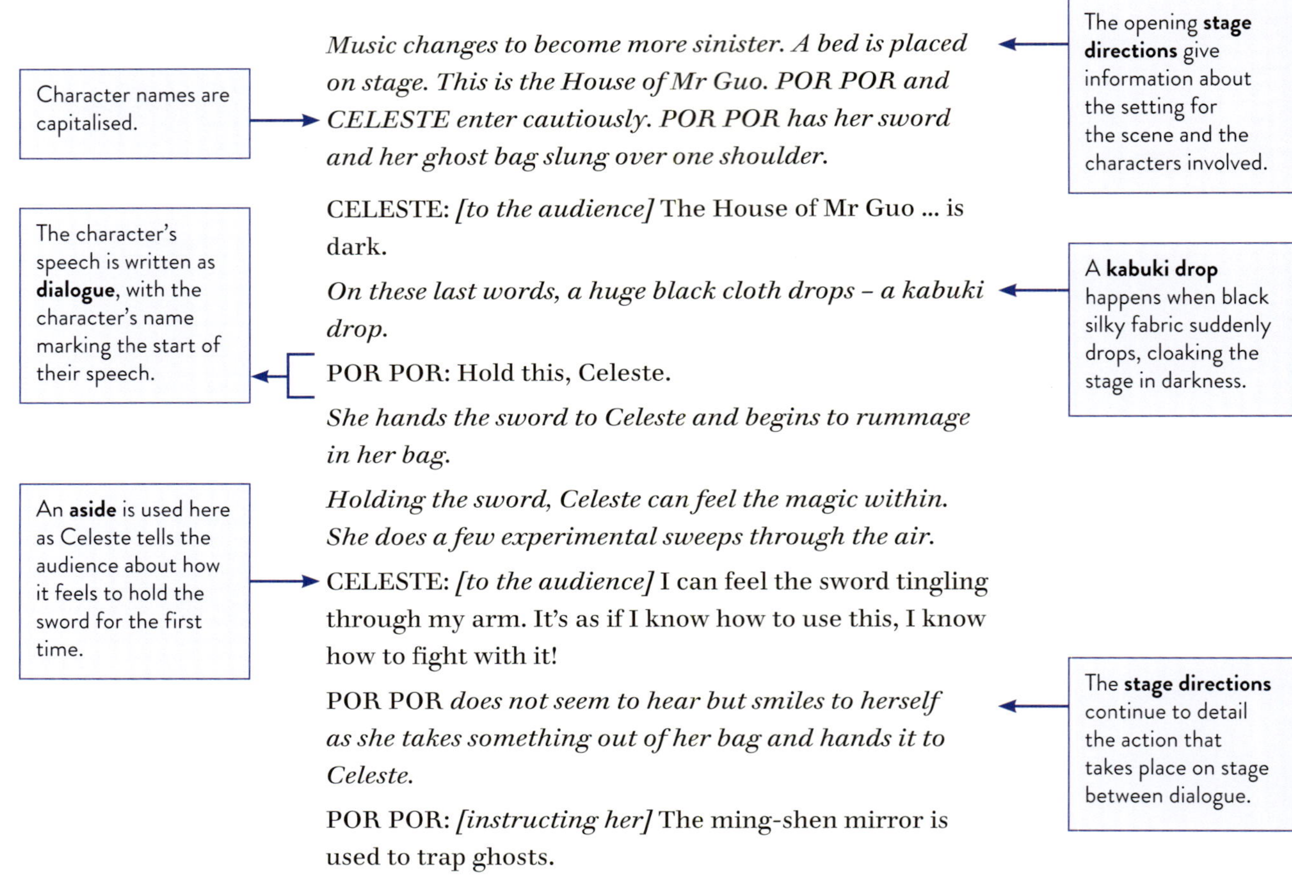

Scene 8. The House of Mr Guo

> The opening **stage directions** give information about the setting for the scene and the characters involved.

> Character names are capitalised.

Music changes to become more sinister. A bed is placed on stage. This is the House of Mr Guo. POR POR and CELESTE enter cautiously. POR POR has her sword and her ghost bag slung over one shoulder.

CELESTE: *[to the audience]* The House of Mr Guo ... is dark.

> A **kabuki drop** happens when black silky fabric suddenly drops, cloaking the stage in darkness.

On these last words, a huge black cloth drops – a kabuki drop.

> The character's speech is written as **dialogue**, with the character's name marking the start of their speech.

POR POR: Hold this, Celeste.

She hands the sword to Celeste and begins to rummage in her bag.

Holding the sword, Celeste can feel the magic within. She does a few experimental sweeps through the air.

> An **aside** is used here as Celeste tells the audience about how it feels to hold the sword for the first time.

CELESTE: *[to the audience]* I can feel the sword tingling through my arm. It's as if I know how to use this, I know how to fight with it!

> The **stage directions** continue to detail the action that takes place on stage between dialogue.

POR POR *does not seem to hear but smiles to herself as she takes something out of her bag and hands it to Celeste.*

POR POR: *[instructing her]* The ming-shen mirror is used to trap ghosts.

Celeste looks at it wonderingly. POR POR *abruptly covers the mirror.*

Ayah! Never look inside the mirror unless a ghost has been captured. If the mirror is empty, you may be trapped within forever.

She finds a little box.

Aha. My ghost revealing powder ... And for you, Celeste ... your weapons.

Celeste's excitement is dampened somewhat as POR POR holds up ... two bells.

> These **stage directions** tell you how the character's dialogue is meant to be performed, giving insight into their feelings.

CELESTE: *[fighting her disappointment]* Bells? No sword?

POR POR: *[smiling]* No sword. Remember: a sword is not always the right weapon for the battle at hand.

2.6.3 Understanding and responding to texts A

1 Summarise what happens in this scene.

2 How do the stage directions create atmosphere and mood for this scene? Give an example to support your response.

3 In her **aside** when she holds the sword, Celeste tells the audience, 'It's as if I know how to use this'. What do you think this tells us about her character?

4 How does the use of asides in this scene make the audience feel involved in the play?

2.6.4 Expressing ideas and composing texts A

How will Celeste fight a ghost with bells? Will she capture the ghost in the mirror?

1 Write the next scene to follow Scene 8. Use the same format as the script here, including stage directions and dialogue.

Extension activity 

Label the **codes and conventions** you have used in your drama script.

How can I be inspired by the style of one playwright to give words a stage?

2.6.5 Understanding and responding to texts B 

You will now closely examine the **style** of Yorta Yorta/Gunaikurnai playwright Andrea James in her drama *Sunshine Super Girl*.

PAUSE: The play *Sunshine Super Girl* tells the story of tennis legend Evonne Goolagong Cawley. Research Evonne's story and culture to learn more about her before you read the extracts below.

VOCABULARY

Style
Style refers to the characteristic ways a writer choses to express their ideas. For a playwright, this may include the way they use elements of the stage, props, lighting and audio-visual features in addition to the way they represent ideas through character, setting and plot.

Setting

The set is a tennis court, orange clay, and a high rise umpire's chair. Some fruit boxes standing on end make do for the players seating. There is a crude string net with an emu feather woven into it here and there. Two clothes lines either end. One line with a big, white bed sheet and the other with a few tiny 1970s tennis dresses and frilly undies fluttering in the air. The audience are seated along two sides in a transverse arrangement.

VOCABULARY

Crude
adjective constructed in a simple, makeshift way.

Transverse
adjective situated across from something.

1 In the space below, draw a picture of how the stage might be set according to this description.

2 Research to find an image of a traditional tennis arena. How is the setting for the play similar and/or different to this image?

3 What do you think the emu feathers woven into the net might **represent** in this play?

Read the following extract from Act 1, Scene 6. In this scene, Mrs Martins, who coached Evonne and her siblings to win the Narrandera Championships, calls Mr Edwards, a Sydney tennis coach.

4 Label the **codes and conventions** used by Andrea James in the blank boxes.

Act 1, Scene 6

A phone rings and MR EDWARDS picks it up. MRS MARTIN, the coach in Barellan, is calling. On each side of the net is a different world. Barellan, hot, orange, windy and dusty; and Sydney, green, lush and luxurious. EVONNE and her TEAMMATES continue the movement drill in Barellan.

MRS MARTIN: Mr Edwards. It's Faith here.

MR EDWARDS: Faith! How's it going at Barellan?

MRS MARTIN: Good! We've got about one hundred kids.

MR EDWARDS: Excellent.

MRS MARTIN: I think there's a young girl here you should come up and see ... There's something about this girl. The way she moves. Her instincts. We'll only be here for two more days. I think you should come out and see her.

MR EDWARDS: Yeah well ...

MRS MARTIN: I think it'll be worth your while, Mr Edwards. You won't regret it.

Pause.

MR EDWARDS: Well, she better be bloody good.

MRS MARTIN: Great!

MR EDWARDS: I'll get Mrs Edwards to reschedule the coaching.

MRS MARTIN: And there's just one more thing?

MR EDWARDS: Hurry up.

MRS MARTIN: The girl?

Beat.

She's dark.

MR EDWARDS: Dark?!

MRS MARTIN: She's an Aboriginal girl.

MR EDWARDS: Ohhhhhh? Interesting ...

2.6.6 Understanding and responding to texts B

1 How does James create two different worlds in this scene? Refer to the stage directions to support your response.

2 What have you learned about Mr Edwards from his dialogue in this scene?

3 What idea do you think James might want to represent in this scene? How does the stage direction 'Beat' help draw the audience's attention to this idea?

2.6.7 Understanding and responding to texts B

Read the following extract from Act 3, Scene 16. In this scene, Evonne competes for the first time at Wimbledon in 1970. Her opponent is Jane 'Peaches' Bartkowicz. The Wimbledon competition is a prestigious tennis tournament in England.

Act 3, Scene 16

REPORTER: Aborigine girl from the outback!

EVONNE: I'm the Wimbledon Freak Show.

EVONNE *prepares to serve. She looks up to the crowd.*

There are 14,000 people seated around this court. Come to watch me play.

EVONNE and PEACHES dance. EVONNE serves and runs in to play; but freezes. She struggles while PEACHES is dancing about brilliantly. The clock and scoreboard click over quickly; 6-4 and 6-0 over 34 minutes. They shake hands at the net and then suddenly EVONNE is seated in front of the press. Bright lights flashing.

PRESS 1, 2 and 3: Miss Goolagong! Miss Goolagong!

PRESS 1: Miss Goolagong! Can you throw a boomerang?

EVONNE: What?

PRESS 3: Miss Goolagong. Do you feel proud to be the first Aborigine to play Wimbledon?

EVONNE: Well ...

PRESS 1: Can you speak Aboriginal?

EVONNE: I ...

PRESS 1: Come on, Evonne, one or two words in Aboriginal.

PRESS 1, 2 and 3: Miss Goolagong! Miss Goolagong!

REPORTER: Dreamtime daughter of the outback crashes in the second round.

The headline 'Dreamtime daughter of the outback crashes in the second round' is projected around the court.

1 Summarise what happens in this scene.

____

____

2 The stage directions indicate that Evonne and Peaches are 'dancing'. Why does James include this as a stage direction?

____

____

3 At the end of the scene, a newspaper headline is projected around the stage. What impact do you think James wants this to have on the audience?

4 Imagine you are the director of a performance of this play. Explain how you would instruct the actors to perform their lines during the press conference part of this scene.

2.6.8 Expressing ideas and composing texts A

Write an author bio for the playwright Andrea James that introduces her style and gives some information about the ideas she represents in her work.

You may like to consider how she uses …

- elements of the stage (including layout, props and visuals) to reflect ideas and set the scene
- unique stage directions to engage the audience
- dialogue to reveal character.

2.6.9 Chapter reflection

1 What have you learned about how drama is a form of oral storytelling?

____

____

____

2 Reflect on one script extract you read in this chapter. Why did this play engage you?

____

____

____

3 What have you learned about the differing styles of various playwrights? For each playwright you examined in this unit, describe their style.

Playwright	Play	Playwright's style
Patricia Cornelius	*Boy Overboard: The Play*	
Mary Morris	*Two Weeks with the Queen: The Play*	
Vanessa Bates	*A Ghost in my Suitcase*	
Andrea James	*Sunshine Super Girl*	

4 Let's return to the unit inquiry question: ***How do spoken texts bring stories and words to life?*** How have your reading experiences in this chapter addressed the inquiry question?

____

____

____

Unit 2: Summative assessment

The summative assessment options below provide opportunities to demonstrate your achievement of the following outcomes and focus areas:

Outcome	EN4-RVL-01 Reading, viewing and listening to texts	EN4-URA-01 Understanding and responding to texts A	EN4-URB-01 Understanding and responding to texts B	EN4-ECA-01 Expressing ideas and composing texts A
Focus Area	Reading, viewing and listening for meaning	Representation Code and convention	Style	Representing Speaking

Option 1:

Inspired by the work of playwrights you have read in this unit, complete the following tasks.

Collaborative

Choose a well-known folktale from your culture or a famous fable, such as one of Aesop's tales. Transform this story into a drama performance.

- Write the drama script, using the codes and conventions of drama.
- Perform a scene of this script for your peers.

Individual

Reflect on your composition.

- As one of the playwrights for this drama, describe your style.
- Discuss how you used unique codes and conventions to develop your style.
- Explain what key ideas you aimed to represent in your drama script. Explain how you used multiple elements within your script to reflect this idea.

Option 2:

Your class will be divided into small groups, which will be called Poetry Slam Circles. Each Poetry Slam Circle will be given a theme or concept as the focus for their poetry. Your teacher can choose this theme, or you can decide as a group what you would like to focus on. Be creative! For example, use the seasons as a focus concept (winter, spring, autumn, summer). Or use opposing themes such as love, hate, justice, revenge.

Individually, compose a poem to be performed for your Poetry Slam Circle that reflects your group's concept or theme.

Be inspired by the performance poems you have read in this unit to plan your choices, including the ...

- key ideas you want to represent through your poem and the way you will create multiple layers of meaning within your poem
- unique style you will use through the choice of codes and conventions.

Watch and enjoy other performers!

Option 3:

Choose any story shared in this unit. Reimagine this story in your own way and compose a text that represents your own version of the story. Choose one of these types of text:

- Poetry – narrative poem, verse novella, performance poem.
- Drama – script for a tragedy, comedy or modern drama.

Perhaps you could reimagine the characters, setting or plot. Keep some elements, change others. Rewrite for a new audience. Add in a new section. Have fun with it!

Annotate your completed composition with notes about how the learning and reading in this unit helped you to reimagine the original story.

Be inspired by texts you have read in this unit to plan your choices, including the ...

- key ideas you want to represent through your reimagining
- unique style you will use through the choice of codes and conventions.

Assessment as learning: self-assessment

Does my composition ...

- ☐ tell a story or share an idea with multiple layers?
- ☐ use the codes and conventions of this form of storytelling?
- ☐ create and maintain a personal style?

What are two strengths of my response?

____

____

What area/s of my response do I need to refine further?

____

____

____

____

UNIT
03

Of beauty, rich and rare

Unit inquiry question:
How are connotation, imagery and symbol used in imaginative texts to help us appreciate our Australian environment?

In this unit, students will explore how imaginative texts use figurative language to represent our natural environment. They will specifically examine how connotation, imagery and symbol are used in imaginative texts to convey images of Australia. Students will closely examine imaginative texts by Australian and Aboriginal and Torres Strait Islander authors – particularly *Blueback* by Tim Winton and *Black Cockatoo* by Carl Merrison and Hakea Hustler – to appreciate the literary value of these texts in reflecting our landscape. By drawing on these texts and their use of figurative devices, students will convey their appreciation for our changing natural landscape by composing their own imaginative compositions.

To address the focus inquiry question of the unit, students will engage with learning in three chapters:

Chapter 7
The land down under

In this chapter, students will be introduced to the ways that connotation, imagery and symbol can be used by writers to convey ideas about the natural landscape. Students will also identify how imaginative texts reflect environmental issues.

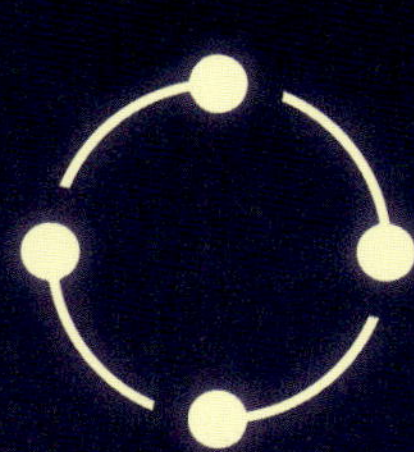

Chapter 8
The depths of the ocean

In this chapter, students will closely examine *Blueback* by Tim Winton. They will investigate how connotation, imagery and symbol are used by Winton to help readers appreciate the sea and acknowledge future environmental concerns. Students will experiment with imagery and symbol in their own imaginative writing.

Chapter 9
The endless sky

In this chapter, students will closely examine *Black Cockatoo* by Carl Merrison and Hakea Hustler as an example of how Aboriginal and Torres Strait Islander authors use figurative language to reflect the world. Students will experiment with narrative conventions to compose an imaginative text that shows an appreciation for Australia's environment.

The learning activities within each chapter and the summative assessment options (on page 147) provide opportunities to assess student achievement of the following outcomes:

Outcome and Focus Area	Content point
EN4-RVL-01 Reading, viewing and listening to texts	**Reading, viewing and listening for meaning**
	Engage with the ways texts contain layers of meaning, or multiple meanings Using a range of texts, describe how Aboriginal and Torres Strait Islander authors convey connections between Culture and identity
EN4-URA-01 Understanding and responding to texts A	**Connotation, imagery and symbol**
	Analyse how figurative language and devices can represent ideas, thoughts and feelings to communicate meaning Explain how Aboriginal and Torres Strait Islander authors use figurative language and devices to shape meaning
	Narrative
	Examine how narratives can depict personal and collective identities, values and experiences
EN4-URC-01 Understanding and responding to texts C	**Literary value**
	Understand how texts from all modes and media can serve different personal, social and cultural purposes according to their form and context Describe how thematic and stylistic qualities of texts contribute to the ways they can be valued in different contexts
EN4-ECA-01 Expressing ideas and composing texts A	**Text features: imaginative**
	Create imaginative texts for creative effect and that reflect a broadening world and relationships within it
	Sentence-level grammar and punctuation
	Make choices about sentence structure or length by constructing a variety of simple, compound and complex sentences for purpose

CHAPTER 7
THE LAND DOWN UNDER

Chapter overview

In this chapter you will consider how the landscape of Australia is reflected in imaginative texts. You will learn about how writers use imagery and symbol to create these images of Australia and experiment with these features in your own writing. You will also examine how imaginative texts can reflect current environmental concerns and issues.

Success criteria: In this chapter, I will be successful when I can ...

- describe how the Australian landscape is shown in texts
- describe how connotation, imagery and symbol create meaning in imaginative texts
- explain how writers use imagery and symbol to represent the Australian landscape
- explain how imaginative texts reflect environmental issues
- use imagery in my own writing to represent the natural landscape.

Chapter inquiry questions

- What does the land down under look like in imaginative texts?
- How do writers use connotation, imagery and symbol to reflect the Australian landscape?
- What environmental issues can imaginative texts reflect?

Key vocabulary

- Imaginative text
- Connotation
- Imagery
- Symbol
- Environmental issue

What does the land down under look like in imaginative texts?

Australia is sometimes called the 'land down under'. The landscape of Australia has been the setting for many different **imaginative texts**, most of which highlight the unique elements of this country.

> **VOCABULARY**
>
> **Imaginative text**
> An imaginative text uses words, sounds or visual images to reflect ideas, feelings and mental images. The aim of an imaginative text is to entertain or to make audiences think about a topic in a new way. Examples of imaginative texts include narrative, poetry, film or picture book. These texts use their elements creatively to engage the audience.

3.7.1 Warm-up

What does 'my Australia' look like?

Photograph, source images or draw the world around you. Create a collage of these images called 'my Australia', to show what this place looks like to you. Share your collage with a small group. Journal your observations of these collages below. What similarities and differences do you notice with other people's versions of 'my Australia'?

____

____

____

____

____

____

3.7.2 Viewing reflection

Visit Australia's national tourism website via the QR code. Although this is not an imaginative text it still gives viewers insights into the landscape of Australia. Look through the website before you respond to the questions below.

1 Describe some of the images of Australia you can see on the website.

____

____

2 Explain how the website creates each of the following impressions of Australia.

Impression of Australia	How does the website show this impression?
A place of adventure	
A social place	
A place of calm and serenity	
A modern and exciting place	

What images of Australia are shown in imaginative texts?

Imaginative texts can use setting to represent images or perspectives of a place. This means that a writer might share a particular idea about a place through the way they describe the setting or what they choose to focus on within the setting.

Australia is a place of many different landscapes, including rural, urban and coastal environments. As a result, there are many different experiences of life in Australia. Imaginative texts help us to appreciate all these experiences and understand what life is like for people all over Australia. You will now examine a range of imaginative texts that show different Australian landscapes.

VOCABULARY

Rural
adjective in, relating to, or characteristic of the countryside.

Urban
adjective in, relating to, or characteristic of a city.

Coastal
adjective of or near the coast.

3.7.3 Reading, viewing and listening to texts

The Australian outback

Some texts celebrate Australia's outback. Look at the film posters on the next page and consider how they compare with your image of the outback.

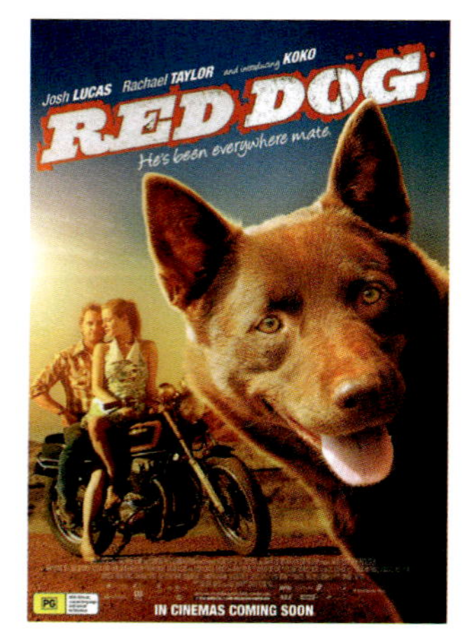		
Red Dog	*Back to the Outback*	*Rabbit Proof Fence*

1 What do these posters suggest about life in the outback?

2 In what similar ways do these film posters reflect the outback?

3 Why do you think people living overseas might imagine Australia this way?

4 Do you think these posters accurately capture life in the outback? Explain your opinion.

3.7.4 Reading, viewing and listening to texts

PAUSE: Before reading the text below, talk with a small group about what you know about rural Australian landscapes. Have you read or viewed any texts that are set in a rural environment?

Rural Australia

The Little Wave by Pip Harry is a verse novel (see information about verse novels in Unit 2: Word of mouth) about a class in Manly, NSW, who invite a country class to the beach for a visit. This extract from the book provides a contrast between rural, urban and coastal Australian landscapes.

The Little Wave

By Pip Harry

We're getting special visitors
this term.

Kids from the bush who
want to swim at Manly.
They're driving a long way,
just for a dip.

Some of them
have never even seen
the ocean. Imagine that!

They're from a town
called Mullin.
We look it up.
Population: 3300.

They've got a post office,
a school
and two rivers.
But no beach.

There are farms there, too.
Wool, wheat and cotton.
But sometimes the drought

is so bad
nothing grows
from the thirsty
cracked earth.

I live in Sydney.
Population: 5.1 million.

1 What landscapes of Australia are mentioned in the text?

____

____

2 What differences are shown between two of the landscapes described in the text? Support your response with evidence from the text.

____

____

3 What does the writer want to show us about life in rural Australia? Support your response with evidence from the text.

3.7.5 Expressing ideas and composing texts A

1 Imagine you are a student in the country class in Mullin and the city kids are coming to your school. Write a poem in the style of the poem above about what you've heard about life in urban Sydney. Use the images of Sydney to inspire you. Begin your poem with the same opening, but reversed.

We're getting special visitors
this term.
Kids from the city **who**
want to see the bush.
Some of them
have never even seen ...

They've got ...

Urban Australia

Over 85% of Australia's population lives in an urban environment. The novel *Laurinda* by Alice Pung opens with a description of a landscape in a fictitious Australian city. In the following extract, the main character reflects on what she and her friend Linh used to see out of the bus window on their way home from school.

Laurinda

By Alice Pung

Remember how we used to catch the 406 bus after school, past the Victory Carpet Factory and the main hub of Sunray, through to Stanley? ... I don't remember what you saw on those bus trips, but this is how I see it now. An old strip of seven shops, each with an identical metallic snake of a roller shutter coiled at the top. At night, with those iron blinds lowered, the street looked like a long, continuous dirty warehouse, all graffiti and concrete.

There was the local fish and chip shop, the Happy Oyster, which had never seen an oyster, joyous or otherwise, from the first day of its existence ... A hairdresser that still called itself a barber, with a red, white and blue pole at the front and posters in the window of great haircuts from 1983.

The largest shop was the milk bar that tried to pass itself off as a mini-mart, with faded packets of instant noodles and tins of soup not seen in a proper supermarket for years.

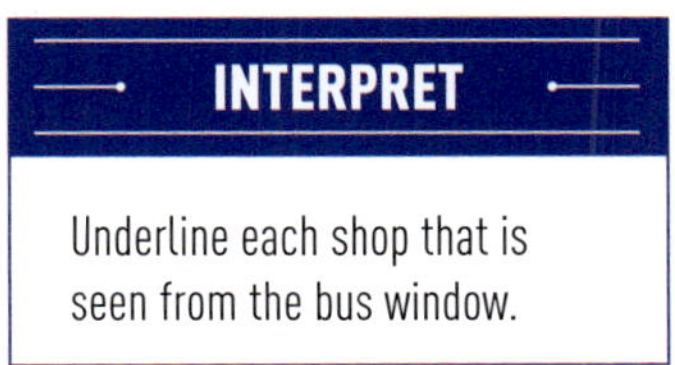

3.7.6 Reading, viewing and listening to texts

1 Draw a picture of the strip of shops that the character can see through the bus window.

2 What does the description of this urban landscape suggest about life in the city?

3 How does this description of the city compare with what you see on your way to and from school?

3.7.7 Reading reflection

1 After reading and viewing the texts above, discuss why you think it is important that there are different and varying images of Australia's landscapes in imaginative texts.

How do writers use connotation, imagery and symbol to reflect the Australian landscape?

One way that writers of imaginative texts create different landscapes of Australia in their writing is through **connotation**, **imagery** and **symbol**. These features are all figurative language devices. Figurative language refers to using words and phrases to mean something other than their literal meaning. By using figurative language the writer helps the reader to create a mental image of what is being described. It can also help the writer suggest or imply another message and meaning within a text.

VOCABULARY

Connotation
A connotation is an implied or suggested meaning that is additional to the basic meaning of what is being presented or described. A connotation can be positive, negative or neutral. As a reader, you draw on your personal experiences to decide the meaning of a connotation. You could also be influenced by the way the connotation is presented.

Connotation

A writer may use **connotation** when describing a landscape to suggest ideas about a place.

Below are two pictures that are of the same house but presented using different colours.

The house in the first picture could have positive connotations of peace and privacy. This is influenced by the bright colours used in the image.

The house in the second picture could have negative connotations of being isolated and detached. The black and white colour scheme may remind viewers of a scary scene from a film.

3.7.8 Understanding and responding to texts A

The following extract is from John Marsden's novel *Tomorrow When the War Began*. The main character, Ellie, describes a mountain ridge called 'Tailor's Stitch' that leads to a remote sinkhole called 'Hell'. Read the description of this part of the Australian bush and consider the connotations used.

Tomorrow When the War Began

By John Marsden

Tailor's, Tailor's Stitch, is a long line, an arete, that goes dead straight from Mt Martin to Wombegonoo. It's rocky, and very narrow and steep in places, but you can walk along it, and there's a bit of cover. The views are fantastic. You can drive almost up on to it at one point, near Mt Martin, on an old logging track that's hard to find now, it's so overgrown. Hell is what's on the other side of Tailor's, a cauldron of boulders and trees and blackberries and feral dogs and wombats and undergrowth. It's a wild place, and I didn't know anyone who'd been there, though I'd stood on the edge and looked down at it quite often. For one thing, I couldn't see how you'd get in there. The cliffs all around it are spectacular, hundreds of metres high in places. There's a series of small cliffs called Satan's Steps that drop into it.

VOCABULARY

Arete
noun a sharp mountain ridge.

LANGUAGE

Circle words that have a positive connotation (i.e. positive descriptions or feelings).

LANGUAGE

Underline words that have a negative connotation (i.e. negative descriptions or feelings).

1 Describe the Australian bushland that is shown in this extract.

2 The remote sinkhole in the middle of Tailor's Stitch is called Hell. What are the connotations of this name and what do you think this suggests about this place?

3 The descriptions of this place use both positive and negative connotations. Complete the table below to explain why the writer does this.

	Words/phrases used	What are the connotations?
Positive		This could be a place of ...
Negative		But it could also be a place of ...

Imagery

Another form of figurative language that a writer may use to reflect part of the Australian landscape is **imagery**.

There are various types of imagery, shown in the figure below.

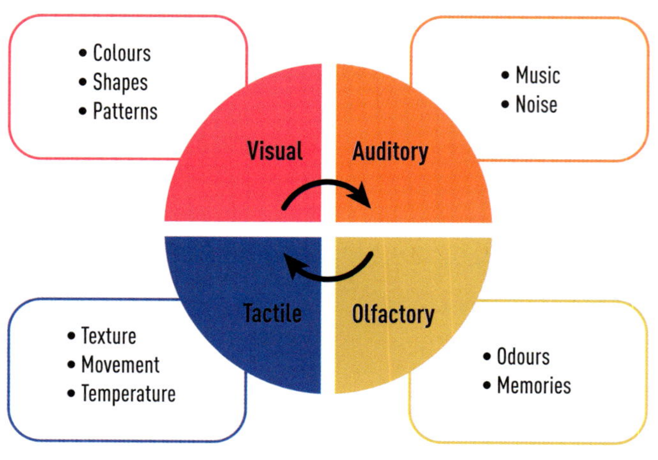

VOCABULARY

Imagery
Imagery occurs when words are used to help readers create a mental image of what is being described, often by activating our senses. This helps us become more engaged with the text and compare it to our own experiences.

Imagery can be created through descriptive language, such as the use of **adjectives** and **adverbs**. Imagery is often also created through other figurative language devices, such as **simile**, **metaphor**, **personification** and **hyperbole**. These features help readers connect their personal experiences to what is shown in a text to better understand a writer's meaning.

3.7.9 Understanding and responding to texts A

Read the poem 'The Forest' by Anna Jacobson and identify examples of imagery used to reflect this part of the Australian landscape.

The Forest

By Anna Jacobson

Silent as a mosquito whine just beyond hearing.
A lizard lies languid, tastes the air with its thick blue tongue.
A goanna runs up a gum tree, claws digging into bark.

A scrub turkey dashes across the path.
I sit on the timber seat halfway up the mountain,
careful of the red-back's nest underneath.

Leaves dance with the first drops of rain. Birds call out.
A tree dribbles sap, sticky as honey. The downpour starts –
I am drenched in the forest's earthy scent.

1 What do you see? Choose one image that you can clearly see and draw a picture of it in as much detail as possible.

2 Identify an example of each type of imagery used in the poem.

Imagery	Example
Visual	
Auditory	
Tactile	
Olfactory	

3 How does imagery help the reader to appreciate the forest as part of our natural landscape?

3.7.10 Expressing ideas and composing texts

From my window ...

Compose a short poem that describes the rural, urban or coastal landscape you can see from your window. Focus on one aspect of this landscape. Use at least **two types of imagery in your poem.**

Symbol

Another way that writers reflect ideas about our world in their writing is by using a **symbol.**

You see symbols every day when you see signs for important places, like the hospital or police station. The colours of traffic lights are symbols that tell you when to stop, slow down or go. Your school uniform is a symbol of your connection to a community.

When you read an imaginative text, always consider if an object has been used to represent a larger idea.

Oodgeroo Noonuccal was an Aboriginal Australian poet and activist. Read her poem '?' and think about what the tree in the poem might symbolise for her culture and identity.

> **VOCABULARY**
>
> **Symbol**
> Writers may use a symbol to represent or show a larger idea, action or feeling. A symbol may be an object, character or place. Usually, a reader draws on what they already know about symbols to make the connection to a larger idea. For example, a setting sun could be a symbol of closure or an ending, while a rising sun is a symbol of a new beginning.

?

By Oodgeroo Noonuccal

Hello tree;
Talk to me.
I'm sick
And lonely.
Are you old?
Trunk so cold.
What secrets
Do you hold? Talk tree!
Can't you see;
My troubles
Trouble me.
Silent tree
Let me see
Your answers.
ANSWER ME.
Tree!
You dare
Question ME?
How dare you
Dare, question ME.

> The poem is written directly to the tree. Discuss with a group what you predict the tree might **symbolise**.

> Noonuccal uses **rhetorical questions** here. The tree cannot answer back, yet the tree has seen the actions of humans for many centuries.

> An **exclamation** is used here to show how we demand so much from our natural environment. This is almost like a command.

> At the end of the poem, go back to your predictions about what the tree may **symbolise**. What new ideas can you add?

3.7.11 Reading reflection

What larger idea do you think the tree is a symbol of in this poem? Consider the poet's context as an Aboriginal and Torres Strait Islander author. What is her relationship with nature and why do you think she wants to share this with her audience?

____

____

____

____

____

What environmental issues can imaginative texts reflect?

Reading imaginative texts that showcase the Australian landscape can help us appreciate our natural environment. These texts can also reveal important environmental issues, such as the destruction of natural resources, climate change and the impact of humans on flora and fauna.

For each of the imaginative texts examined in this chapter, identify a possible environmental issue shown in the text. Support your ideas with evidence from the text.

Text	Environmental issue	Textual evidence
The Little Wave		
Laurinda		
Tomorrow When the War Began		
The Forest		
?		

Extension activity

A popular **genre** of young adult fiction is dystopian fiction. Texts within this genre are often set in a future where the world has been destroyed in some way or people have a terrible way of life due to restriction or oppression. Writers may use these texts to warn readers about something in our current society that needs to be looked after.

Read the following extract from Bren MacDibble's dystopian novel *How to Bee* about a world in which bees are extinct and children work as bees to maintain the ecosystem.

How to Bee

By Bren MacDibble

Today's lesson's just for us. It's about the history of the bees. Not us. The real ones they used to have thirty years ago before the famines.

I think they looked like pests. Not the kids who kill pests but the actual bugs. They flew on little wings like some pests from flower to flower to collect nectar to make something sweet like sugar to share with people. 'Honey,' the speaker says over and over, like honey was the whole point of bees, not this job I'm doing now. I don't know what honey tastes like. Gramps knows. He says, 'Sweet like honey,' sometimes. When the real bees flew from flower to flower, they did this job. One tiny bee could do the work of twenty kid bees every day. And the speaker says there used to be millions of them.

I think all the bees went away coz they looked small like pests. Before the famine, farmers didn't have enough farm kids to catch the pests so they sprayed poison on the pests, but the poison didn't know which was bees and which was pests.

Scientists still have some of the little bees and they say one day they'll bring them back to work on the farms.

1 Research other Australian dystopian novels that focus on environmental issues.

2 Why do you think this is a popular genre of fiction?

3 What can we learn from these texts?

4 Prepare a presentation for your peers.

3.7.12 Chapter reflection

1 Explain two images of the land down under that were shown in the texts you examined in this chapter. Support your answer with evidence.

Image of Australia	How did a text show this image?
A place of ...	
A place of ...	

2 Give your own definitions of **connotation**, **imagery** and **symbol**, supported by examples from texts you read in this chapter.

	My definition	Textual example
Connotation		
Imagery		
Symbol		

3 Let's return to the unit inquiry question: ***How are connotation, imagery and symbol used in imaginative texts to help us appreciate our Australian environment?*** How have your reading experiences in this chapter addressed this inquiry question?

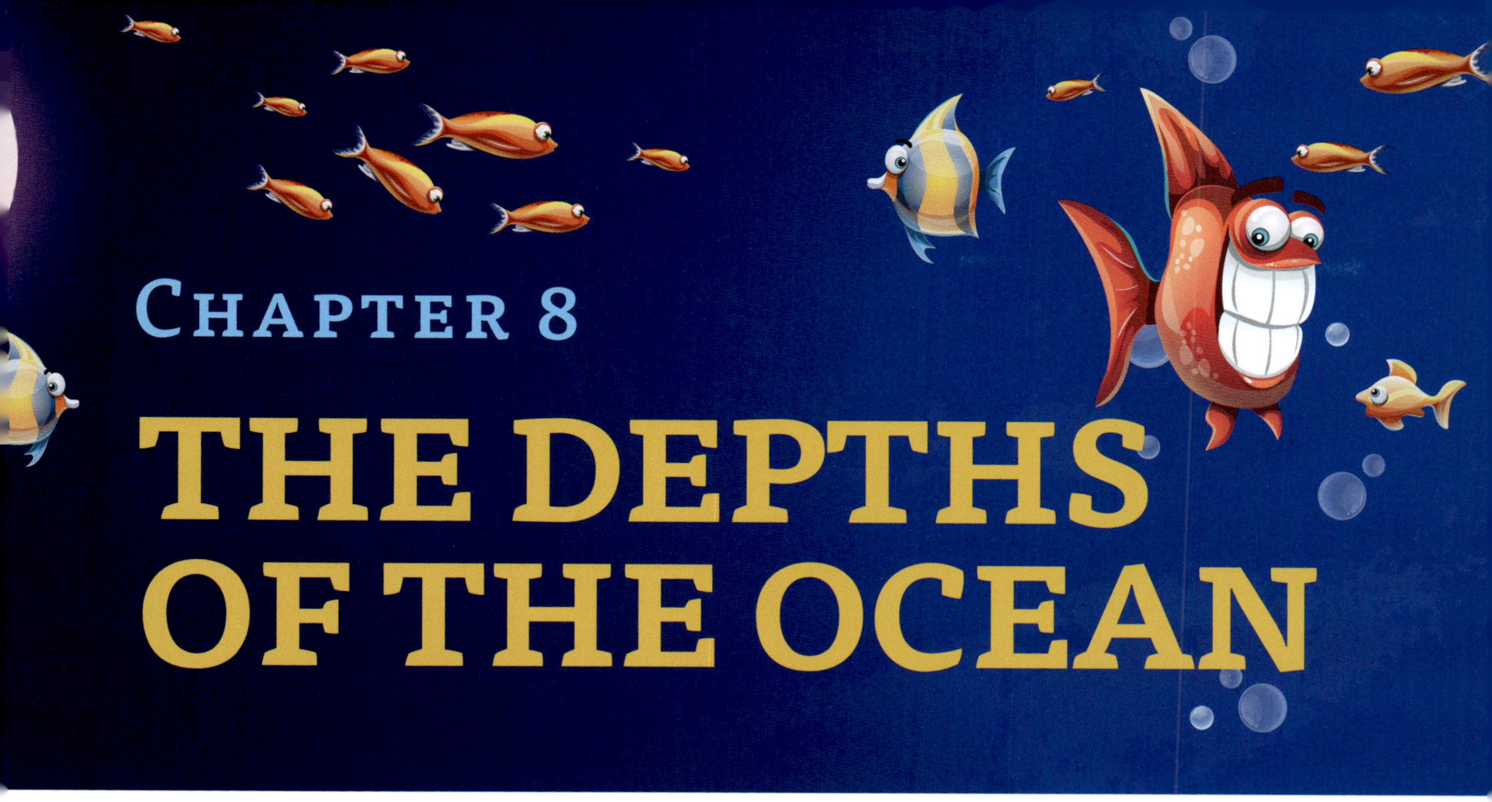

CHAPTER 8

THE DEPTHS OF THE OCEAN

Chapter overview

In this chapter, you will closely examine the novel *Blueback* by Tim Winton. You will investigate how imagery and symbol are used by Winton to help readers appreciate the ocean and acknowledge future environmental concerns. You will experiment with imagery and symbol in your own imaginative writing.

Success criteria: In this chapter, I will be successful when I can ...

- identify the codes and conventions of a narrative
- identify examples of imagery and symbol in *Blueback*
- describe how Winton uses the codes and conventions of a narrative to communicate ideas about the environment
- explain how imagery and symbol are used in *Blueback* to engage readers and show ideas about the environment
- explain the literary value of *Blueback* for audiences
- use imagery and symbol in my own writing to represent aspects of the environment.

Chapter inquiry questions

- What does the narrative of *Blueback* show about the environment?
- How are imagery and symbol used in *Blueback* to help us appreciate the ocean?
- How can I write with imagery and symbol to reflect our relationship with nature?

Key vocabulary

- Narrative
- Environmental sustainability
- Appreciation
- Literary value

What does the narrative of *Blueback* show about the environment?

Blueback is a novel written by Australian author Tim Winton. The story is set in a small coastal village called Longboat Bay and follows the life of Abel Jackson and his mother, Dora. When he is a young boy Abel meets a blue groper fish, who he calls Blueback. As the story progresses, we see Abel grow into adulthood and as he gets older he learns more about how to respect the ocean. However, he also witnesses those who do not appreciate the beauty of the ocean and its creatures, and he learns about the selfish nature of humans. Although Abel moves away from his home by the ocean, whenever he returns he visits his old friend Blueback. Woven into the life story of Abel, the narrative shares some important ideas about the environment.

3.8.1 Warm-up

Connotations of the ocean

What do you think of when you look at each of the images below? Write one connotation of the ocean for each of the images. Think about what the image makes you feel or think about. Is it positive or negative?

Hint: Go back to Chapter 7 if you need a reminder about connotations.

What are the codes and conventions of a narrative?

Let's recap your knowledge of the **codes and conventions** of a **narrative**.

Structure

Structure, or narrative structure, is the ordering or sequence of events in a story.

The 'three-act structure' of a story – comprising a beginning, a middle and an end – goes back to Ancient Greek plays. It's the most basic and well-known structure for novels and film scripts, and our brains are wired to appreciate and feel satisfied by stories that follow this structure.

Gustav Freytag, a German novelist, developed Freytag's Pyramid, a visual representation of this three-act structure.

The 'beginning, middle and end' structure can also be called the 'set-up, conflict and resolution' or the 'exposition, climax and denouement'. They all refer to the same basic structure.

> **VOCABULARY**
>
> **Narrative**
> A narrative is the communication of a story made up of a sequence of events. A narrative shares a message or idea that invites us to see the world differently.
>
> **Codes and conventions**
> Remember, codes and conventions are the arrangement of language features and structures specific to a form of text that help create meaning. The codes and conventions help you recognise and create familiarity with the type of text you are reading.

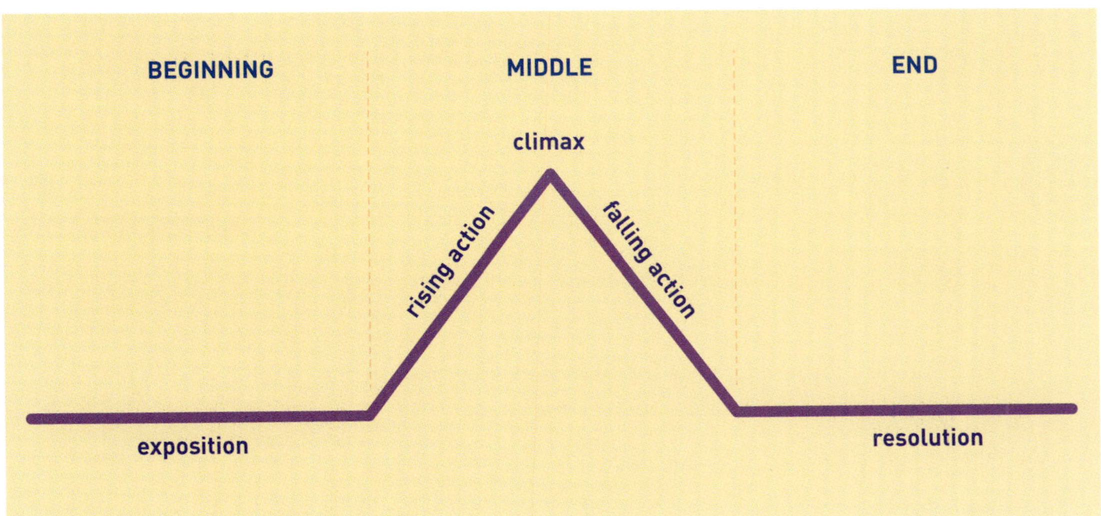

The beginning of the story sets up the exposition (introduction) of the characters and setting. The rising action builds towards a crisis or climax.

The middle of the story details the crisis or climax (the moment of greatest dramatic tension), which is the turning point of the story.

The falling action shows the consequences of the middle turning point and ties the story up in the resolution at the end.

3.8.2 Reading texts

Blueback follows the traditional narrative structure. However, Winton also structures the novel by focusing on major events in different stages of Abel's life: childhood, teenage years, young adulthood, adulthood and fatherhood.

What do you think is effective about structuring a novel in this way?

____

____

____

Extension activity

Not all narratives follow the traditional structure listed above. Some narratives subvert or change this structure. For example, the narrative may begin with a complication or leave an ending unfinished. Discuss with a peer:

What stories do you know of that subvert or change the traditional narrative structure?

Plot

Plot refers to the series of events that make up a story and fall within the structure of the narrative.

3.8.3 Reading texts

Here is a list of events from the plot of *Blueback*. Label the graph below using the numbers from the list.

1. Abel and his mother Dora live by the ocean. They live off the ocean by fishing for abalone but only ever take as much as they need.
2. Abel meets Blueback, a blue groper fish.
3. Mad Macka, a local fisherman, dies of a heart attack while fishing.
4. Costello's fishing boat arrives. Abel investigates and discovers Costello's over-fishing practices.
5. Costello attempts to spear and kill Blueback, but he is scared away by Dora and Abel.
6. Businessmen arrive at the bay with plans to construct a resort.
7. Abel leaves the bay to study and work as a Marine Biologist.
8. Dora is successful in her to petition for the bay to be saved.
9. Abel returns to the bay with his wife to look after Dora and decides to stay to look after the bay.

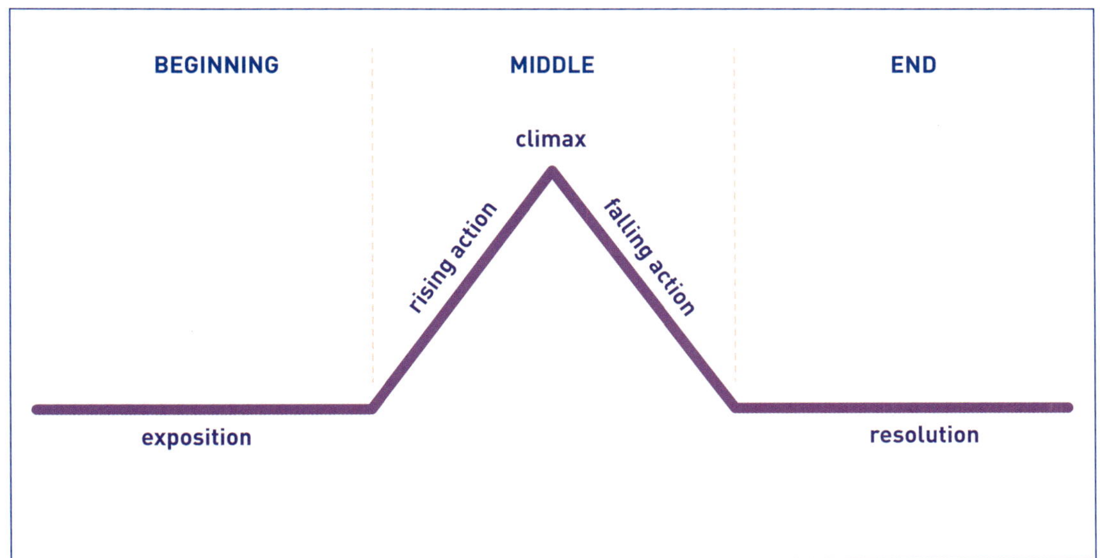

Extension activity

The novel's blurb describes *Blueback* as a 'deceptively simple allegory'. However, the story has also been described as a fable.

1 Research the meaning of both **allegory** and **fable.** Look at well-known examples of each to help you understand these types of stories.

2 Research the plot of *Blueback* in more detail. What could the plot and ideas of the narrative reflect more deeply than literal events?

3 Pick a position – is this an allegory, fable or just a well-written narrative? Justify your choice.

Setting

The **setting** within a narrative is the time and place where the events of the story occur. The time of the setting refers to the social or historical period of the narrative. The place of the setting refers to the geographic location. *Blueback* is set in the fictional town of Longboat Bay in Western Australia. The Jacksons have lived at the bay for many generations. Abel and Dora live without electricity and are quite isolated from other people.

3.8.4 Expressing ideas and composing texts A

Find some images online of coastal bays in Western Australia. Use **visual imagery** to describe what it would be like to live in a remote location like this.

____

____

____

____

____

Characters

Characters are the people within a story that help readers connect with the ideas of the narrative. The main character of a story is called the **protagonist**. Readers usually connect with the protagonist, depending on the point of view used by the writer. A writer may use different characters to share differing perspectives and to illustrate their main ideas.

> **VOCABULARY**
>
> **Visual imagery**
> To create visual imagery, focus on describing what can be seen – for example, colours, size or shape. You could also compare what is seen to something else (using a simile or metaphor) to help your reader create a mental image.
>
> **Hint: Go back to Chapter 7 for a more detailed reminder about imagery.**

3.8.5 Reading texts

Read the following extract from Blueback.

Blueback

By Tim Winton

Abel Jackson had lived by the sea here at Longboat Bay ever since he could remember. His whole life was the sea and the bush. Every day was special, his mother always told him this, but it all became much more precious the day he first shook hands with old Blueback.

What have you learned about the following characters from this extract?

- Abel:

____

____

- Dora:

____

____

Theme

A **theme** is a message or idea shared by a narrative through the plot, setting and characters. Themes may invite readers to think about a topic or issue in a particular way or see the world differently. For example, the Harry Potter series by JK Rowling conveys a theme of bravery. The series shows us that true bravery stems from loyalty, friendship and facing your fears.

Some key themes of Tim Winton's *Blueback* are listed below.

Environmental sustainability	Family	Growing up
The beauty of nature	Belonging	Greed

Environmental themes of the novel

A significant theme of *Blueback* is **environmental sustainability**. This means that we all have a responsibility to protect our natural resources and look after the environment. The novel invites readers to think about the respect we have for the natural environment, like the ocean and all the creatures that live in the ocean. Abel and Dora are careful to only take from the ocean what they need, which is a natural part of the cycle of life. However, other characters, like Costello, act with greed and show disrespect to the environment.

3.8.6 Reading texts

Below are some issues raised through the theme of environmental sustainability in the novel. Research each issue to understand the themes in more detail. Then explain why these are environmental concerns.

Issue	How does the text reflect this?	Why is this an environmental concern?
Overfishing	Abel discovers that Costello has taken more than a fair share of abalone from the bay, plus he finds other fish recklessly gutted on Costello's boat.	
Land development	Businessmen arrive at Longboat Bay to develop the land into a resort and tourist attraction.	

Extension activity

Read this extract of the epigraph written at the beginning of the novel. An epigraph is a collection of quotes or phrases at the beginning of a text, which often signal the writer's purpose or message. What do you think this epigraph suggests about the novel's key message about environmental sustainability?

... As for us:
We must uncentre our minds from ourselves;
We must unhumanise our views a little, and become confident
As the rock and ocean that we were made from.

Robinson Jeffers, 'Carmel Point'

How are imagery and symbol used in *Blueback* to help us appreciate the ocean?

A key characteristic of the novel *Blueback* is Winton's use of imagery and symbol. Winton's purpose for writing *Blueback* is for readers to develop an appreciation for the ocean. To have an **appreciation** for the ocean is to respect its place and role in the natural environment and aim to protect it as an important resource.

You will now read extracts from the text and examine the ways imagery and symbol are used to help readers connect with the beauty of the ocean.

Blueback

By Tim Winton

Abel fell back into the water with a cold crash. A cloud of bubbles swelled around him, clinging to his skin like pearls. Then he cleared his snorkel – pfft! – and rolled over to look down at the world underwater.

Great, round boulders and dark cracks loomed below. Tiny silverfish hung in nervous schools. Seaweed trembled in the gentle current. Orange starfish and yellow plates of coral glowed from the deeper slopes where his mother was already gliding like a bird.

Abel loved being underwater. He was 10 years old and could never remember a time when he could not dive. His mother said he was a diver before he was born; he floated and swam in the warm ocean inside her for nine months, so maybe it came naturally.

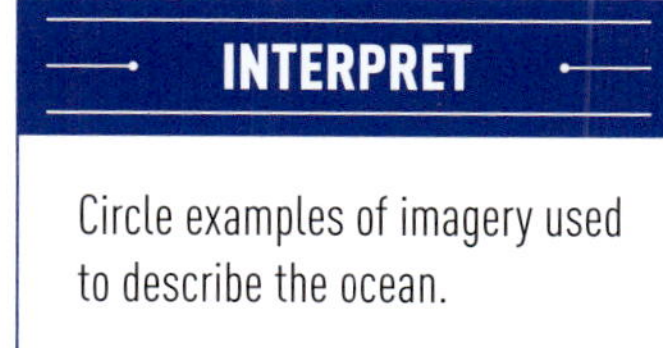

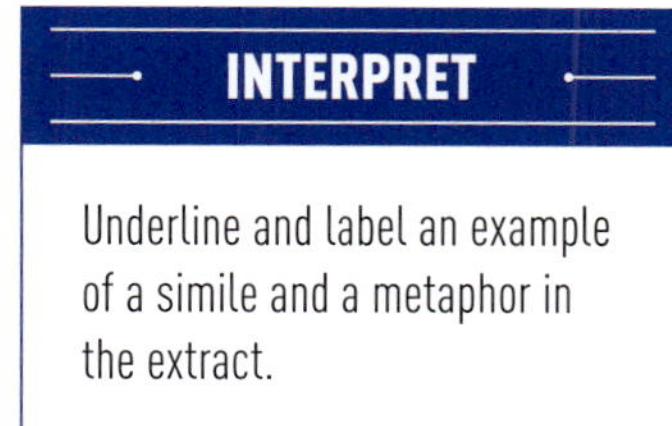

3.8.7 Understanding and responding to texts A

1 List three examples of imagery used in this extract and explain what each shows about Abel's relationship with the ocean.

Hint: Go back to Chapter 7 if you need a reminder about imagery.

Examples of imagery	What does this show about Abel's relationship with the sea?

Expressing ideas and composing texts A

Where is somewhere that you feel the same way Abel feels in the ocean? Describe yourself in this place.

___

___

___

___

___

___

___

___

___

___

Blueback as a symbol

When Abel first meets Blueback he is scared because of his size. However, he learns that he is quite playful and likes Abel's attention. Abel spends a lot of his time with Blueback as a child and visits him again whenever Abel returns to the bay as an adult.

Blueback

By Tim Winton

Abel and his mother slid down into the deep again and saw the fish hovering then turning, eyeing them cautiously as they came. It twitched a little and edged along in front of them to keep its distance. The big gills fanned. All its armoured scales rippled in lines of green and black blending into the dizziest blue. The groper moved without the slightest effort. It was magnificent; the most beautiful thing Abel had ever seen.

After a few moments his mother eased forward with an abalone in one outstretched hand. The groper watched her. It turned away for a moment, afraid, and then it came around in a circle. Abel couldn't hold his breath much longer but he didn't want to miss anything so he hung there above his mother and the fish with his lungs nearly bursting.

The groper arched back. The mosaic of its scales shone in the morning sun. His mother got close enough to touch the fish with the meat of the abalone. The fish trembled in the water and then froze for a moment as though getting ready to flee. She ran the shellmeat along its fat bottom lip and let go. The fish powdered forward, chomped the abalone and hurtled off into the dark deep hole.

... 'I can't believe it,' said Abel. 'It's big enough to eat your arm off.'

'He must be old to grow that big,' said his mother as she pulled on the starter rope.

'He's so blue.'

'And smart,' she said. 'He knew what he was doing. We're lucky, you know, lucky to see such a thing.'

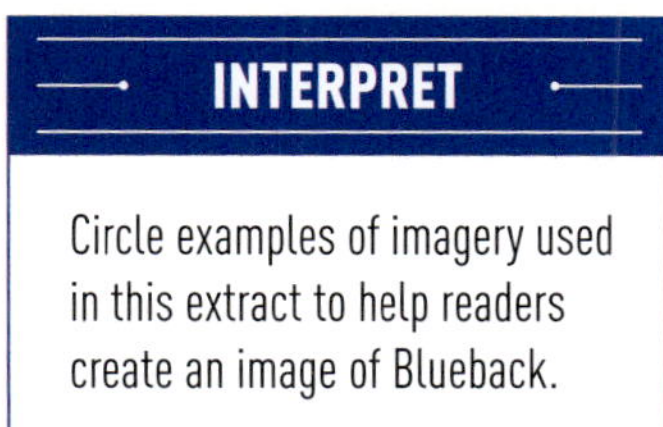

INTERPRET

Circle examples of imagery used in this extract to help readers create an image of Blueback.

3.8.9 Understanding and responding to texts A

1 How does Winton use imagery to help create an image of Blueback for readers? Support with textual evidence.

____

____

2 Look closely at the following quotations from this extract. What do you think Blueback symbolises about nature in each quotation?

Hint: Go back to Chapter 7 if you need a reminder about symbols.

Quotations	What does this symbolise about nature?
'It was magnificent; the most beautiful thing Abel had ever seen.'	
'It turned away for a moment, afraid, and then it came around in a circle.'	
'"And smart," she said. "He knew what he was doing. We're lucky, you know, lucky to see such a thing."'	

Human greed symbolised

Tim Winton uses the character of Costello to symbolise human greed. Costello takes more than his fair share of abalone from the bay, showing disrespect for nature, and he shows greed as he aims to profit from overfishing. Read the following extract about the death of the tiger shark to see how Winton has symbolised human greed in the novel.

Blueback

By Tim Winton

A huge tiger shark swam into the bay. Abel took his boat out to see the thing swimming sluggishly up and down the beach. ...

The shark looked wrinkled and flabby when it should have been thick and powerful as a tree. It wasn't hard to see why. Everywhere it went it towed a big red buoy on a length of chain. It had a stainless-steel meat hook in its jaws and it swam like a ghost of itself. The shark couldn't dive without being defeated by the buoy and dragged painfully back to the surface. The day it was hooked it would have dragged it underwater for hours but now its strength was gone and every turn of its head, every kick of the tail was agony. The buoy dragged behind like a ball on a chain. The tiger shark was starving to death and dying of exhaustion. It was a pitiful sight and it sickened Abel. If he'd had a gun he would have pulled alongside and shot it through the head to end its suffering. There was no way he could save the shark now, even if he could cut it free.

So, Abel watched the shark all afternoon. In the end he came ashore and watched it from the jetty. It swam feebly up and down, restless with its terrible agony. That night he sat on the verandah and saw moonlight flash on the dragging buoy which made a miserable sparkling wake on the still water.

In the morning the tiger shark was dead. The tide left it stiff and leathery on the beach and Abel turned the red buoy over in his hands to see the name stencilled on the side. COSTELLO.

He towed the shark out to sea, replaced the buoy with some lead weights and cut it free. It sailed down into the black deep like a torpedoed ship.

Abel went back to school in the new year feeling older, different. That summer he learnt that there was nothing in nature as cruel and savage as a greedy human being.

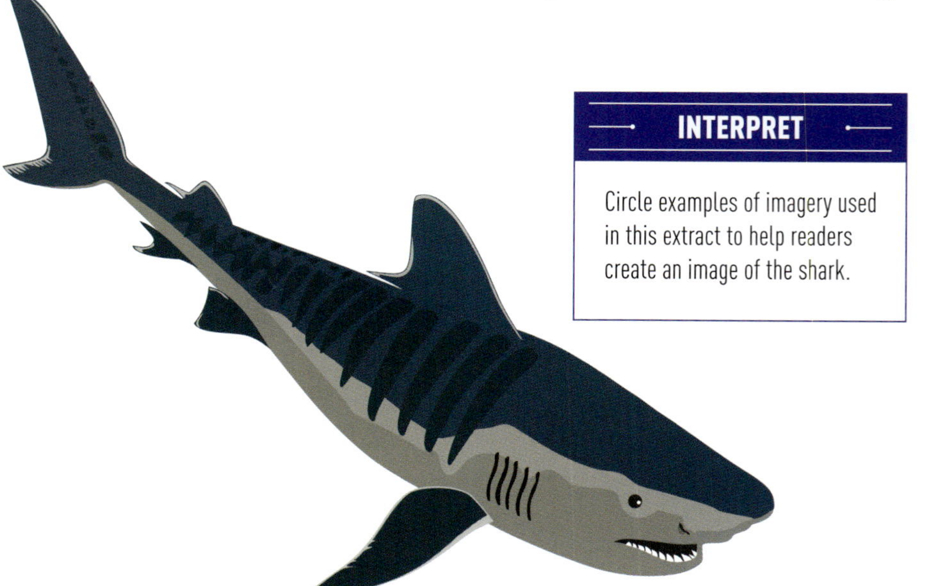

INTERPRET

Circle examples of imagery used in this extract to help readers create an image of the shark.

INTERPRET

Underline an example of a simile used in this extract.

Hint: A simile is a comparison between two things using words such as *like* or *as*.

3.8.10 Understanding and responding to texts A

At the end of this extract, it is said that Abel 'learnt that there was nothing in nature as cruel and savage as a greedy human being'. Explain how Winton uses the shark in this extract to symbolise the idea of human greed.

Literary value of *Blueback*

A text has **literary value** if it raises important questions about aspects of our world and the way we live. Literary value also means that a text is relevant for many groups of people and draws out ideas that we all need to consider.

3.8.11 Understanding and responding to texts C

From your examination of the themes, imagery and symbols of *Blueback*, why do you think this text has literary value?

How can I write with imagery and symbol to reflect our relationship with nature?

It is now your turn to write with imagery and symbol like Tim Winton! He writes about the ocean because this is a significant part of his personal context. Winton grew up in Western Australia by the beach and has a great passion for the ocean. What aspect of nature do you appreciate?

3.8.12 Expressing ideas and composing texts A

Just as Abel meets Blueback and is instantly in awe of his magnificence, you are to write a section of a narrative when a character encounters an aspect of nature. This could be an encounter with an animal, a weather event, an unexpected discovery in nature, gardening, gazing at stars, watching birds or a simple walk.

Use imagery and symbol in your writing to invite readers to appreciate this aspect of nature.

PAUSE: First, you must plan your composition.

Aspect of nature:

____

Encounter:

____

Character:

____

Symbol:

____

Type/s of imagery to use (circle one): visual / auditory / tactile / olfactory

Other codes and conventions:

____

____

Write your narrative here:

____

____

____

____

____

____

3.8.13 Chapter reflection

1 Select another narrative you have recently read or viewed. Describe the codes and conventions for this narrative.

Narrative title:

Codes and conventions	Description
Structure	
Plot	
Setting	
Characters	
Themes	

2 Create a summary of Winton's writing style in *Blueback*. Describe how he uses imagery and symbol to invite us to appreciate the environment.

Write your summary below or create a multimodal presentation (images, music and text).

3 Let's return to the unit inquiry question: ***How are connotation, imagery and symbol used in imaginative texts to help us appreciate our Australian environment?*** How has your study of *Blueback* in this chapter addressed the inquiry question? Support your response with textual evidence.

Chapter 9
THE ENDLESS SKY

Chapter overview

In this chapter, you will investigate how Aboriginal and Torres Strait Islander authors use figurative language to reflect their appreciation of nature and connection to the land. Inspired by this reading, you will experiment with narrative conventions to compose an imaginative text that shows an appreciation for Australia's environment.

Success criteria: In this chapter, I will be successful when I can ...

- describe connotations of symbols used in *Black Cockatoo*
- describe the relationship between Aboriginal and Torres Strait Islander peoples and the land
- explain how contrast is used to reflect important ideas
- explain how imagery and symbol are used in *Black Cockatoo* to engage readers and show ideas about the environment
- explain the ways in which *Black Cockatoo* has literary value
- compose my own narrative to reflect my appreciation for the Australian environment.

Chapter inquiry questions

- How do Aboriginal and Torres Strait Islander authors use imagery and symbol to show their connection to the land?
- How can I show my appreciation for the Australian environment through narrative?

Key vocabulary

- Reciprocal
- Contrast
- Colour imagery
- Literary value

How do Aboriginal and Torres Strait Islander authors use imagery and symbol to show their connection to the land?

For Aboriginal and Torres Strait Islander peoples the land, or Country, is of great importance. Country is central to Aboriginal and Torres Strait Islander cultures, the centre of spiritual identity. For tens of thousands of years, the land has served Aboriginal and Torres Strait Islander peoples as a source of food, water, shelter and spirituality; Country is respected as a living person. The relationship between people and the land is **reciprocal**, which means that people do not only take from the land, but they also have a responsibility to look after it and give back to it too.

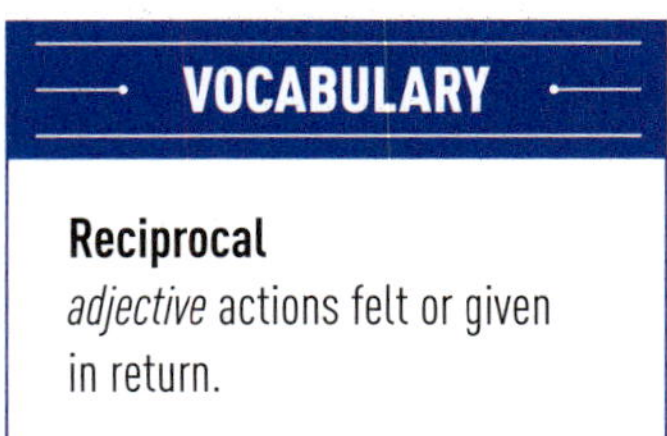
VOCABULARY

Reciprocal
adjective actions felt or given in return.

3.9.1 Warm-up

Connotations of freedom

What does freedom in nature look like to you? Create a collage of images of our natural environment that have the connotation of freedom. Share your collage with a peer and compare your connotations.

Hint: Go back to Chapter 7 if you need a reminder about connotations.

Extension activity

Create a collage of images of nature that have connotations of restriction, captivity or confinement. Share your collage with a peer and discuss:

- Why are the connotations of these images different from your first collage?
- From each collage, what one image best symbolises each connotation?

There are many Aboriginal and Torres Strait Islander stories that share the story of creation. You can read and view some of these stories in Chapter 4 of this workbook. In these stories, Country is central to creation. Sharing these stories about the land has also given Aboriginal and Torres Strait Islander peoples a sense of community and family.

PAUSE: Use this QR code to learn more about Aboriginal and Torres Strait Islander connection to Country. Discuss what is meant by the following quote:

'We do not own the land rather the land owns us.'
– Dennis Foley, Gai-mariagal and Wiradjuri man and Fulbright scholar

In this section of the unit, you will investigate how Aboriginal and Torres Strait Islander authors use figurative language, including imagery and symbol, to show their connection to Country. You will also learn how readers are invited to appreciate the land through Aboriginal languages and ways of sharing stories. To illustrate these points, you will closely examine extracts from *Black Cockatoo* by Carl Merrison and Hakea Hustler.

How does *Black Cockatoo* by Carl Merrison and Hakea Hustler show an appreciation of the land?

In *Black Cockatoo*, 13-year-old Mia rescues a black cockatoo after it is hurt by her brother, Jy. Mia keeps the cockatoo in her bedroom until she finds a cage for the bird, to protect it and give it time to heal. She must also hide the cockatoo from her brother and his friends, who have shown cruelty towards other animals too. Mia struggles to understand why her brother has disconnected himself from their family and their culture. Mia also reflects on her connection to culture and the feeling that she is torn between two worlds as she wishes to one day leave and explore the world.

PAUSE: The story is written from an Aboriginal person's perspective. Research the authors to learn more about their life and consider how this might help them create an Aboriginal voice in the text.

Hint: Go back to Unit 1 for a reminder about writing with voice.

Using Aboriginal and Torres Strait Islander languages

Aboriginal and Torres Strait Islander authors may use Aboriginal and Torres Strait Islander languages in their writing to share their culture and reflect their connection to Country.

The Jaru language is spoken in the Kimberley region of Western Australia. *Black Cockatoo* uses Jaru alongside English. Below is a glossary of some of the Jaru words used in the text and their English translation.

Jaru	English	Jaru	English
Barranga	Late dry season and build-up to the wet	Jarrambayi	Sand goanna
Dirrarn	Black cockatoo	Jawiji	Grandfather/grandchild
Gunyarr	Dog	Murnduj	Black-headed python

3.9.2 Reading texts

1 Look closely at this glossary list. These Jaru words and all others used in the text relate to either people or the natural environment. What does this suggest about the importance of nature to Jaru culture?

____

____

2 Research another Aboriginal and Torres Strait Islander language. List some words for parts of nature in this language and their English translation.

____

____

____

Contrasting views of culture

Mia and Jy are shown to have contrasting views and appreciation of their culture.

Mia listens to the stories of her *jawiji* (grandparents) as they share their Aboriginal culture. However, Mia feels that Jy is disconnected from this culture and doesn't show an appreciation for his family.

Read the following extract from the opening of the text.

VOCABULARY

Contrast
Contrast is used by writers to show differences between two or more subjects, people, places or ideas. Showing these differences can help the writer emphasise a key idea or desirable quality. For example, in *Charlotte's Web*, the spider Charlotte is shown to be patient, clever and caring while Templeton the rat is presented as sneaky and untrustworthy. This contrast highlights the qualities we desire in our friends.

Black Cockatoo

By Carl Merrison and Hakea Hustler

The hit came hard, sending the young *dirrarn* black cockatoo reeling from his roost in the large gum tree. The boy approached cautiously, shanghai dangling from his hand, to inspect his catch. The dirrarn lay sprawled amongst the smaller birds he'd been using as target practice.

'Jy! I hope you are planning to eat that one, at least,' said Mia, looking at the devastation at the bottom of the yard.

Jy whirled around, shanghai loaded. 'Get lost, nobody asked you.'

Mia bent down, scooped up the dirrarn, cradled it to her chest and walked defiantly back inside, tears in her eyes.

'We don't just kill for the fun of it, *jawiji* grandson,' said Jy's grandfather as he walked onto the verandah, cup of tea in hand. His calm presence insisted that he be heard.

'Nah, I was just practising, *jawiji* grandfather,' Jy said, head bowed respectfully. 'It was just some fun.'

VOCABULARY

Shanghai
noun slingshot.

INTERPRET

Using two different coloured pens, underline examples that show a contrast between Mia and Jy's actions towards the cockatoo.

3.9.3 Reading texts

1 Explain what happens in this extract.

____

____

2 'The dirrarn lay sprawled amongst the smaller birds he'd been using as target practice.'

a What image is created through the word 'sprawled'? Hint: Search for a definition of this word if you are unfamiliar with its meaning.

____

____

b What does 'target practice' suggest about Jy's relationship with nature?

____

____

3 How does this extract show the **reciprocal** relationship between Aboriginal and Torres Strait Islander people and the environment? Support your answer with textual evidence.

4 How are Mia and Jy **contrasted** in their views towards the bird in this extract? Support your answer with textual evidence.

Black cockatoo as a symbol

The dirrarn is an important symbol used throughout the text. We learn that this animal is Mia's totem, which is an important connection between people and the environment in many Aboriginal and Torres Strait Islander cultures.

PAUSE: Research the meaning and significance of totems in Aboriginal and Torres Strait Islander cultures.

Write your understanding here:

Read the following extract in which Mia's grandfather explains to her how the black cockatoo became her totem.

Black Cockatoo

By Carl Merrison and Hakea Hustler

As they settle down around the fire waiting for their dinner to cook, Mia's jawiji sat close and began telling a story in a hushed tone.

'Before you were born, Mia, I took your father out hunting. It had been a proper long *barranga* dry weather, so to hunt we didn't have to travel far to find big fat *bin.girrjaru* bush turkey. Your father spotted that bin.girrjaru in the shrub and looked at him. As the spear flew through the air, the breeze caught our smell and that bin.girrjaru took flight, disturbing some dirrarn that were hunting on the ground. The spear hit a dirrarn and killed him. You have his mark, Mia, between your shoulderblades. The dirrarn is your totem. Your *jarriny* totem.'

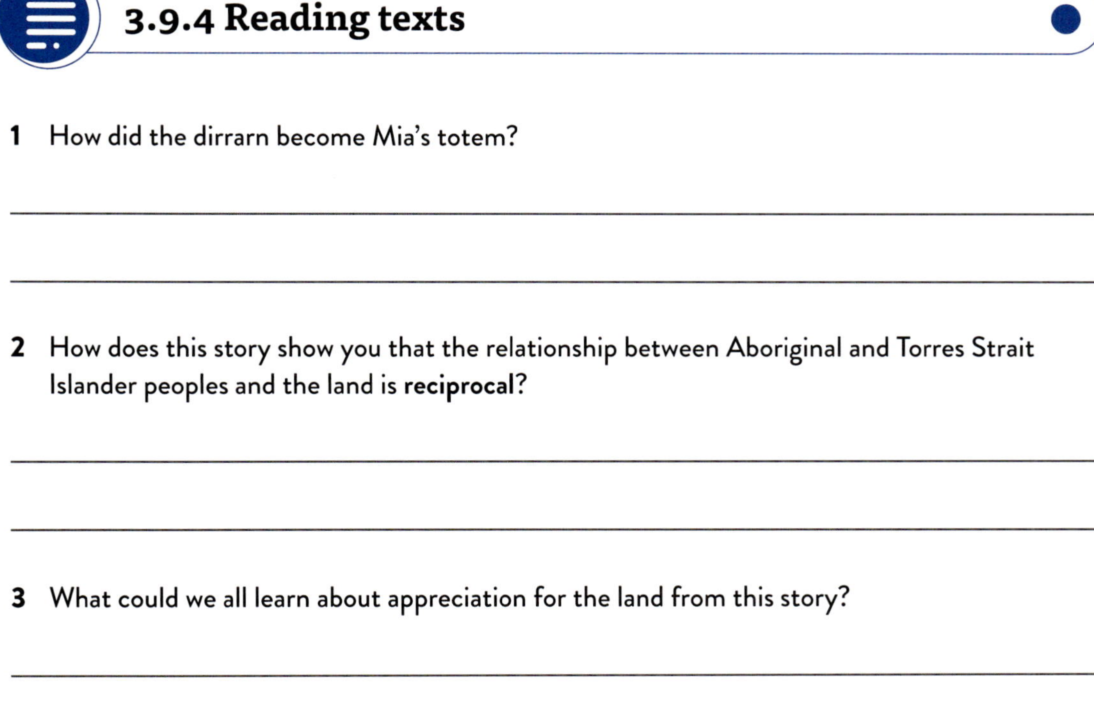

3.9.4 Reading texts

1 How did the dirrarn become Mia's totem?

____

____

2 How does this story show you that the relationship between Aboriginal and Torres Strait Islander peoples and the land is **reciprocal**?

____

____

3 What could we all learn about appreciation for the land from this story?

____

____

Throughout the story, Mia attempts to help the cockatoo recover from its injuries. She locks it in a cage to protect it from her brother and his friends. At the same time, Mia struggles with her own desire to explore the world beyond her home. She feels that she shouldn't leave home to explore the world as she may lose connection with her family and culture. Mia feels as though she is in two worlds.

Throughout the text, there are references to flying and the writers use **imagery** to describe these experiences of flying.

PAUSE: With a group, discuss the **connotations** of flying. Consider what comes to mind and what emotions are associated with flying.

Hint: Go back to Chapter 7 if you need a reminder about connotations.

In the following extract, from the beginning of the text, Mia describes her home in Western Australia. **Colour imagery** is used by the writers to help readers imagine this scene.

Black Cockatoo

By Carl Merrison and Hakea Hustler

Mia let her mind wander to all the places she had dreamt of seeing. No one in her family had left the west coast, let alone travelled over oceans. In days past there was no need to, the family had everything they needed on their country. She imagined soaring high above the coastline, red cliffs below, as the waves crashed onto golden shores – even in her imagination she could not fly out over the waves.

VOCABULARY

Colour imagery
Colour imagery involves describing colours in a scene to allow readers to create a mental image. Colours can also be used symbolically to reflect emotions or draw associations from the reader. Certain colours can have connotations, for example yellow has the connotation of happiness while darker colours may have more serious connotations. Some colours have multiple connotations, like red which can be associated with both passion and danger. Other clues within the text are needed to determine the intended connotation.

3.9.5 Expressing ideas and composing texts A

In this extract, the writers focus on what Mia can see as she imagines herself flying over her home in Western Australia. **Colour imagery** is used as the writers focus on the colours Mia can see, for example 'red cliffs' and 'golden shores'.

Find an image of another aspect of Australia's natural environment (for example, rainforest, remote bushland, mountain ranges). Write a description of this scene as you imagine yourself flying above it. Use colour imagery as the writers do in the extract.

In the final chapter, Mia dreams that she is flying. Read the extract below and consider how the writers use **imagery** to describe what she sees.

Black Cockatoo

By Carl Merrison and Hakea Hustler

Mia dreamt she was flying. She had a sense of freedom and felt the force of the wind under her wings. She saw many places over vast distances; the red-lined rises of giant worn mountains; round large boulders that dotted the landscape; the rich, green path of swollen riverbeds. She enjoyed the freedom and the company of her kind as they rested in trees and soared on the breeze. Mia laughed wildly with them by waterholes and kept a respectful distance between herself and her fellow winged beings. She also flew higher into the sky as the red sun warmed her feathers.

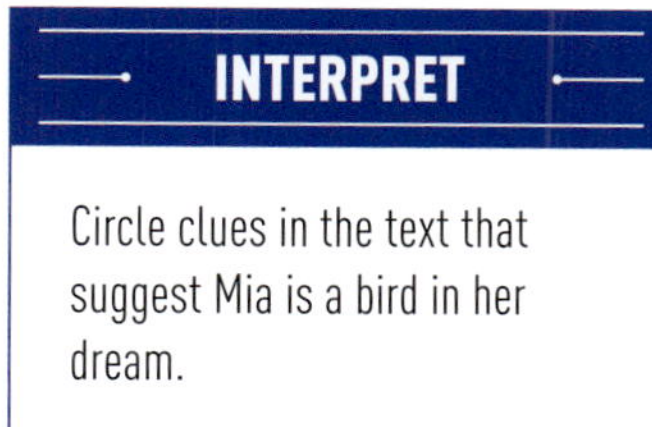

3.9.6 Understanding and responding to texts A

1 List the sights that Mia can see in her dream.

2 In this dream, Mia imagines herself as a bird flying freely. What does this **symbolise** about how she is feeling in real life?

3 How does **colour imagery** in this extract help readers appreciate the natural environment?

PAUSE: Sentence-level grammar and punctuation.

Writers use various types of sentences to draw out different responses from the reader. This has been illustrated in the previous extract. Let's recap your understanding of types of sentences with examples from the extract.

Sentence type	Explanation	Example from extract
Simple	Contains one independent clause (a main piece of information).	Mia dreamt she was flying.
Compound	Contains two independent clauses (which could be sentences on their own). These clauses are joined by a **coordinating conjunction** (words like 'and', 'but', 'so' and 'or').	She had a sense of freedom **and** felt the force of the wind under her wings.
Complex	Contains a main piece of information (which could be a sentence on its own) called **the main clause**, and some extra information (that could not be a sentence on its own) called the subordinate clause.	**She saw many places over vast distances; the red-lined rises of giant worn mountains; round large boulders that dotted the landscape; the rich, green path of swollen riverbeds.**

Notice how in the extract example, imagery is built through the complex sentence. A semi-colon (;) punctuation mark is used in this complex sentence to create a list of the images Mia sees as she imagines herself flying. In this list we learn that Mia can see mountains, boulders and riverbeds. These scenes are all described in more detail in this complex sentence.

3.9.7 Expressing ideas and composing texts A

Go back to the description you wrote in Activity 3.9.5. In different colours underline any simple, compound or complex sentences that you used.

Now, rewrite this description to include more variety in your sentences. Challenge yourself to use complex sentences to build imagery.

In the final chapter, Mia comes to the realisation that she must release the dirrarn from its cage so it can be free. This action has great **symbolism**. Read the following extract from the ending of the text.

Black Cockatoo

By Carl Merrison and Hakea Hustler

Mia stared at her captive. She gently reached into the cage, carefully avoiding the strong beak and sharp claws. Slowly Mia untied the cloth strips that held the wings in place. She watched as the dirrarn slowly stretched his fragile wings. She knew he would not last long in the bush, outside the safety of his cage, but Mia knew it was right. She left the cage door open, gave a silent nod and walked away. A strong wind stirred up red dust around her and she could feel the dirrarn's freedom.

3.9.8 Understanding and responding to texts A

1 Mia knows the bird will not survive in the wild, but she still lets it free. What does this **symbolise** about her appreciation of nature?

2 Throughout the text, Mia is worried that if she 'flies away' or leaves her home she will lose connection with her culture. What does the action of freeing the bird **symbolise** about her own life?

Literary value of *Black Cockatoo*

Remember, a text has **literary value** if it raises important questions about aspects of our world and the way we live.

VOCABULARY

Literary value
Literary value means that a text reflects important ideas for our society. It also means that the text and its ideas are relevant for people from different contexts and may encourage readers to reflect on their own life and values.

3.9.9 Understanding and responding to texts C

From your examination of the themes, imagery and symbols of *Black Cockatoo*, why do you think this text has literary value?

How can I show my appreciation for the Australian environment through narrative?

In this chapter, you have learned about Aboriginal and Torres Strait Islander authors using figurative language to reflect their connection to nature. In other chapters, you have learned about writers use the codes and conventions of narrative to also help readers appreciate the environment.

You will now plan and write part of a narrative that shows your appreciation for the Australian environment.

3.9.10 Expressing ideas and composing texts A

PAUSE: First, you must plan your composition. What aspect of the Australian environment do you want to show an appreciation of?

Aspect of nature:

____

Purpose (what do you want readers to appreciate?):

____

____

____

Codes and conventions of your narrative

Who is the protagonist?

____

What is the complication?

____

Where is the setting?

____

What is the plot?

____

On the visual below of a narrative structure, plot the events you listed above. Then circle the part of the narrative you will write.

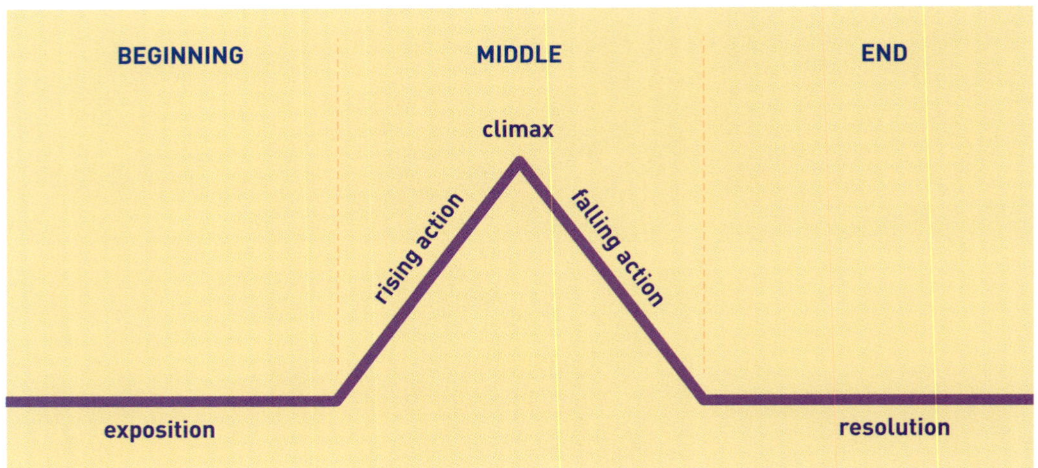

Connotation, imagery and symbol

Choose a symbol to use in your narrative:

____

How will this symbolise your main idea?

____

What are the connotations of this symbol?

____

Type/s of imagery to use (circle one): visual / auditory / tactile / olfactory

Sentence-level punctuation and grammar

Plan how you will use different sentence types.

Sentence type	How will I use this type of sentence?
Simple	
Compound	
Complex	

Write the section of your narrative here:

3.9.11 Chapter reflection

1 What have you learned about how Aboriginal and Torres Strait Islander authors invite readers to appreciate the natural environment?

2 What other texts (books, films, poems) can you find that focus on an animal to reflect an idea about the environment?

3 What are your strengths and areas for improvement as an imaginative writer?

4 Let's return to the unit inquiry question: ***How are connotation, imagery and symbol used in imaginative texts to help us appreciate our Australian environment?*** How has your study of *Black Cockatoo* in this chapter addressed the inquiry question? Support your response with textual evidence.

Unit 3: **Summative assessment**

The summative assessment options below provide opportunities to demonstrate your achievement of the following outcomes and focus areas:

Outcome	EN4-RVL-01 Reading, viewing and listening to texts	EN4-URA-01 Understanding and responding to texts A	EN4-URC-01 Understanding and responding to texts C	EN4-ECA-01 Expressing ideas and composing texts A
Focus Area	Reading, viewing and listening for meaning	Connotation, imagery and symbol	Literary value	Text features: imaginative
		Narrative		Sentence-level grammar and punctuation

Option 1:

Blueback by Tim Winton is structured by the stages of Abel's life, yet we see him return to Longboat Bay and Blueback at all these stages. Inspired by this text, write two chapters of a narrative that features the same protagonist at two different stages of life and shows their connection with nature.

Be guided by the following questions to plan and write your response.

- What aspect of nature will the text celebrate and appreciate?
- How is your protagonist connected to this aspect of nature?
- What stages of life will you show in your chapters?
- What connects these two stages of life within your story?
- What **symbol/s** can you use in both chapters to highlight an aspect of nature?
- How can you use **connotation and imagery** in your writing to help readers appreciate nature?
- How will you use the **codes and conventions of narrative** to show your main idea?
- How can you write with a **variety of sentences** to engage your reader?

Option 2:

Black Cockatoo by Carl Merrison and Hakea Hustler uses contrast between Mia and Jy to show different views of nature. Inspired by this text, write an imaginative response that shows how two different characters contrast in their appreciation of nature.

Be guided by the following questions to plan and write your response.

- What aspect of nature will the text celebrate and appreciate?
- How do your characters contrast in their appreciation of this aspect of nature?
- What connects these characters to this experience of nature?
- What **symbol/s** can you use to highlight an aspect of nature?
- How can you use **connotation and imagery** in your writing to help readers appreciate nature?
- How will you use the **codes and conventions of narrative** to show your main idea?
- How can you write with a variety of sentences to engage your reader?

Option 3:

Choose one of the texts examined in this unit. Compose an imaginative piece that **reimagines** this story and its ideas in your own way. Consider the following ideas and questions.

- Change the setting – where else could the text be set (location or time) to share the same message?
- Reimagine the characters – how could the story be different if the characters were different somehow?
- Add in a new section – is there something missing from the original text that you need to include to further emphasise the main idea?
- Another symbol – can another animal symbol be substituted to show another appreciation of nature?

Annotate your complete composition with notes about how the learning and reading in this unit helped you to reimagine the original story.

Be inspired by texts you have read in this unit to plan your choices, including the way you use:

- the codes and conventions of narrative
- connotation, imagery and symbol
- a variety of sentences to engage readers.

Assessment as Learning: Self-Assessment

Does my response:

- ☐ tell a story or share an idea about nature with multiple layers?
- ☐ use the codes and conventions of narrative?
- ☐ use connotation, imagery and symbol?
- ☐ use a variety of sentences for differing purposes?

What are two strengths of my response?

____

____

____

What area/s of my response do I need to refine further?

____

____

____

UNIT 04

Kids these days

Unit inquiry question:
How do the themes and language of film texts celebrate teens?

In this unit, students will explore how the themes and language of film texts reflect important ideas about teens. They will be introduced to the language of film and consider the ways this language is used to convey themes about youth. Students will also be introduced to the concept of intertextuality as they consider how representations of the teenage experience have developed over time. A close examination of the film *The Hunt for the Wilderpeople* and other film texts will enable students to consider how modern texts celebrate the role of teens in society. Students will communicate their own ideas about how film texts celebrate teens by composing analytical and informative responses, drawing on texts viewed throughout the unit.

To address the focus inquiry question of the unit, students will engage with learning in three chapters:

Chapter 10
Teens in texts

In this chapter, students will identify and describe themes about teens reflected in texts. They will be introduced to the concept of intertextuality and consider how representations of teens have developed over time and for different contexts.

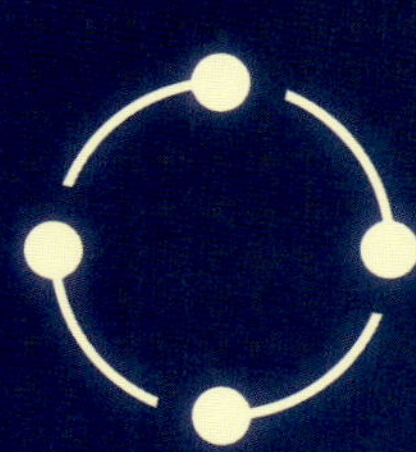

Chapter 11
The hunt for the modern teen

In this chapter, students will learn the language of film to analyse how themes are reflected in film texts. Students will closely examine the film *The Hunt for the Wilderpeople*, directed by Taika Waititi. They will analyse how film language is used to convey themes about the modern teen experience.

Chapter 12
Challenging stereotypes to celebrate youth

In this chapter, students will further analyse how modern films challenge stereotypes of youth in order to celebrate the role of teens in society. Students will learn how to communicate their ideas in analytical and informative responses.

The learning activities within each chapter and the summative assessment options (on page 192) provide opportunities to assess student achievement of the following outcomes:

Focus Area	Content
EN4-RVL-01	**Reading, viewing and listening for meaning**
Reading, viewing and listening to texts	Explore the main ideas and thematic concerns posed by a text for meaning Explain personal responses to characters, situations and issues in texts, recognising the role of written, oral or visual language in influencing these personal responses
EN4-URB-01	**Theme**
Understanding and responding to texts B	Understand how repetition, patterning and language features used within a text communicate ideas about social, personal, ethical and philosophical issues and experiences, and demonstrate this understanding through written, spoken, visual and multimodal responses
EN4-URC-01	**Intertextuality**
Understanding and responding to texts C	Analyse how texts can draw on elements of other texts to enrich meaning Understand how and why texts can be adapted, appropriated or transformed for different contexts, purposes and audiences, and experiment with adaptations, appropriations and transformations in own work
	Literary value
	Describe how thematic and stylistic qualities of texts contribute to the ways they can be valued in different contexts
EN4-ECA-01	**Text features: informative and analytical**
Expressing ideas and composing texts A	Compose texts that include a detailed introduction of ideas, the logical progression of supporting points, and a rhetorically effective conclusion, which reflect a broadening understanding of facts, concepts and perspectives beyond immediate experience
EN4-ECB-01	**Planning, monitoring and revising**
Expressing ideas and composing texts B	Integrate information and perspectives from different sources to create detailed and informed texts Develop a coherent thesis for extended analytical and persuasive texts that represents logical thinking about a text or topic

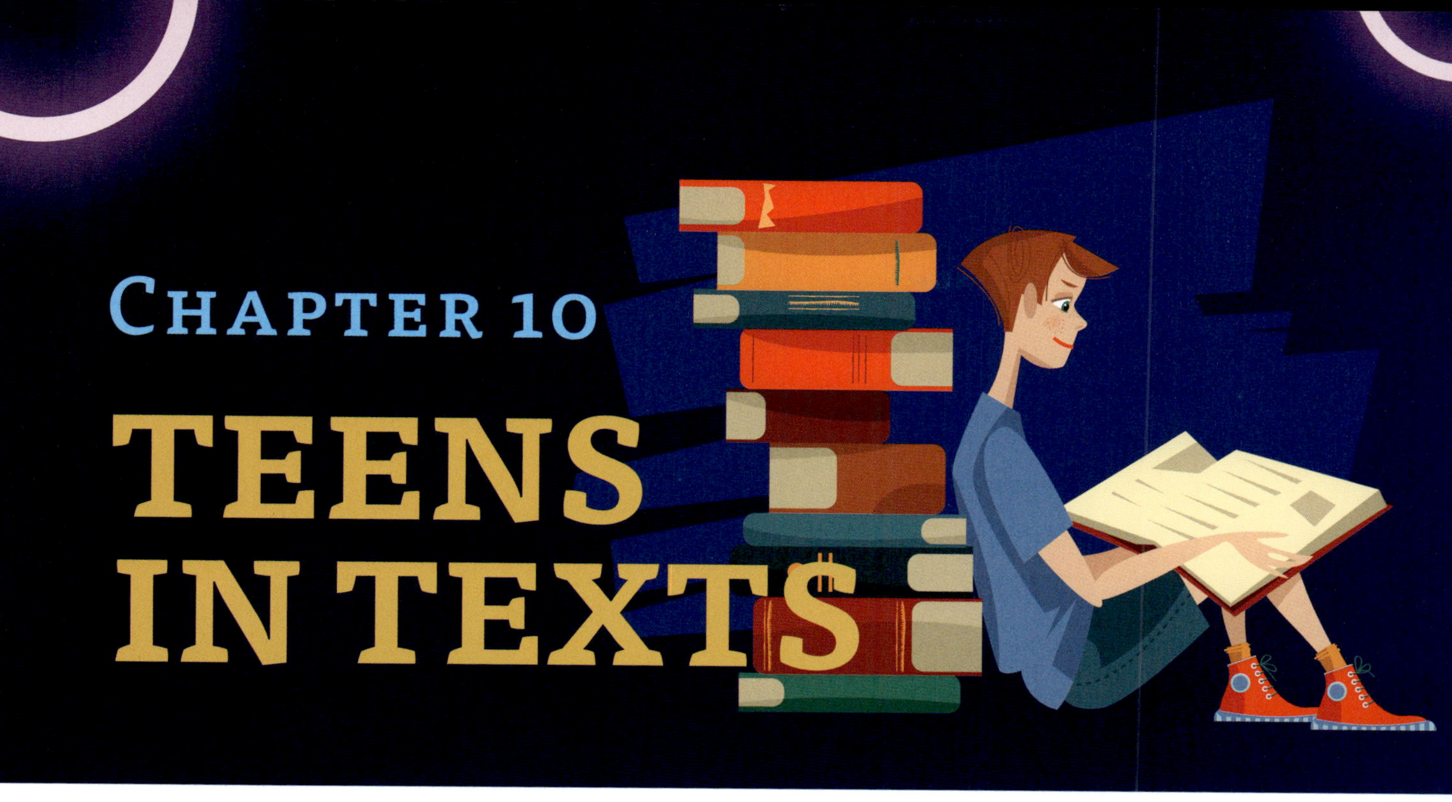

Chapter 10
Teens in Texts

Chapter overview

In this chapter you will consider how themes about teens are reflected in both written and film texts. You will also examine how these themes have developed over time and have been recreated in modern texts.

Success criteria: In this chapter, I will be successful when I can …

- identify themes about teens reflected in texts
- describe how themes about teens in texts have developed over time
- discuss how themes about teens have been appropriated in different contexts
- compose analytical responses to communicate my ideas
- share my personal views on the issues faced by teens today.

Chapter inquiry questions

- What is a theme in a text?
- What themes do texts reflect about teens?
- How have themes about teens been appropriated in texts for different contexts?

Key vocabulary

- Theme
- Analytical response
- Intertextuality
- Context
- Appropriation

What is a theme in a text?

You of all people know what it is like to be a teen as you are living this experience right now. But what do texts reflect about being a teenager? In this chapter you will examine how texts reflect **themes** about the teen experience.

4.10.1 Warm-up

What do the stats say about teens?

Research statistics and information about Australian teens.

- What percentage of the population are teens?
- What issues do teens face?
- What are the physical, emotional and mental health statistics for teens?
- What about education and work?
- How are teens engaged in the community? What else can you research about life as a teen in Australia?

Create a visual representation or infographic to share the main findings from your research.

Extension activity

To deepen your research, you could also ...

- survey your peers and/or teens in other year groups. Do the statistics you have researched match the experiences of teens in your immediate environment? What differences can you see?
- identify texts you have read or viewed that show some of the experiences you have researched above about life as a teen.

What is a theme?

First, let's understand what themes are and why texts reflect them.

The themes of a text are more than the topic of a text or the ideas it may reflect. Consider the process below to help you determine the themes of a text.

VOCABULARY

Theme
A theme may be seen simply as the message or moral of a story or text. A theme may also be described as a writer's attitude or belief about a certain topic, presented as a statement about life.

What is the **topic** of the text? → What **idea** is shown about the topic? → What **statement or point** is the writer making about this topic and idea?

Let's look at the film *Mulan* as an example and apply the process above.

Topics	Ideas	Themes
Family Tradition War Gender	Loyalty Honour Strength Femininity/masculinity	True strength is found when you accept your most complete self. The most honourable characteristics are courage and compassion.

Themes in a text invite the audience to reflect on their own attitudes and values. For example, after viewing *Mulan* you may feel more confidence in your own sense of self, or you may reconsider the ways that you connect with your cultural traditions.

What themes do texts reflect about teens?

You will now examine what kinds of themes about teens and teenage life are reflected in some different texts.

PAUSE: Before continuing, try making some predictions. What types of experiences do you think are commonly reflected about teens in texts? Why do you think this?

Discuss your predictions in a small group.

First, let's have a look at some **written texts** to examine what themes are reflected about teens.

Read the extracts below and complete Activity 4.10.2.

August & Jones

By Pip Harry

It's blustery and cold, wind whipping through my thin footy jersey. The ball is headed my way. I try to unstick from my player, but he's like glue. My legs are muddy, and my knee throbs from tripping while trying to catch a kick from our captain, Rafferty Brown, and ending up sprawled on the ground like a squashed insect.

'Move the ball, boys!' Dad shouts from the sideline, where he's pacing, agitated. He glances at me and rolls his eyes.

'Find some space, August, for goodness sake!'

Parents are not supposed to yell from the sidelines, there's a sign that says so, but my dad is the coach, so it's his job.

He's been yelling at me on a regular basis since I was a little kid in Auskick and now I'm in the Lane Cove Cats Under 12s team. At home, he makes me do drills with my older brother, Archer, in the backyard or down at the park ... I bring a book, but Dad usually confiscates it and makes me focus on the field. *Learn something from the professionals. See what real teamwork looks like.*

INTERPRET

Circle words in the first paragraph that show that playing AFL is an unpleasant experience for August.

LANGUAGE

Discuss with a peer what the indirect speech (written in italics) tells you about the relationship between August and his dad.

Mikki and Me and the Out-of-Tune Tree

By Marion Roberts

I was feeling gloomy about Sylvie, who up until then I'd thought was my best friend.

There was absolutely no denying that ever since school had broken up, when Sylvie had 'accidentally' left me off the socials group for the beach gathering, she'd been acting super weird. I was slowly starting to put all the puzzle pieces together. Sylvie didn't invite me back to her place after the silent disco in the school hall either, then pretended it was just another mistake. Did she think I wouldn't notice? In a small town like Kingfisher Bay everyone notices everything, believe me!

LANGUAGE

Discuss with a peer why inverted commas are used for the word 'accidentally'. What does this show about the character's feelings?

4.10.2 Understanding and responding to texts B

1 What emotions are shown in these extracts that could be experienced by other teens?

2 How do you feel when you read about each character's experience in the texts?

3 What is one theme reflected in each extract about life as a teenager?

Now, let's compare the themes shared in these written texts with **film texts**.

▶▶ *Find and watch the 'Lunch Room' scene from the film* A Monster Calls *directed by JA Bayona.*

4.10.3 Understanding and responding to texts B

1 Describe the experience shown in this film clip.

2 Is the Monster real? If not, what do you think he might reflect?

3 What themes do you think this film might suggest about emotions experienced by teens?

▶▶ *Next, watch the short film* One Small Step *by TAIKO Studios and then complete the 'See, Think, Wonder' activity.*

4.10.4 Viewing texts

What do you *SEE* about the experience of being a teen in this film?	What themes about teens does this film make you *THINK* about?	Can you *WONDER* how these themes might be relevant for other teens in other situations?

You have read and viewed how themes about teens are reflected in some written and film texts. Now it is time to consider how these reflections of teens are similar. You will learn below how to produce an **analytical response**, drawing on the texts you have read or viewed in this section of the chapter.

VOCABULARY

Analytical response
An analytical response shares a perspective by presenting logically sequenced ideas. Usually, in this type of response you look closely at the ideas of the texts, including the way they are structured and written. In your response you will draw out your own ideas and support these with evidence from the texts.

4.10.5 Expressing ideas and composing texts A

Explain how the texts you have read and viewed in this section of the chapter share a similar theme about the experience of being a teenager.

Use the scaffold below to compose your **analytical response**.

Structure of response	Language to use	Write your response
Topic sentence: Identify a similar theme from the texts about the experience of being a teenager.		
Explanation: Explain why this is a common theme and how this relates to the teen experience.	**Cause and effect**: *because, as a result of, consequently*	
Textual evidence: Discuss how at least two texts you have read or viewed show this theme. Ensure you introduce the texts.	**Comparative**: *similarly, also, alike, in the same way*	
Personal response: Do you think this theme is accurate about the teen experience? Give your opinion.	**Evaluative**: *effective, accurate/ inaccurate, appropriate/ inappropriate*	

How have themes about teens been appropriated in texts for different contexts?

Have teens always been presented in the same way that you have just seen in the texts so far? You will now investigate how texts can be created for different time periods to share similar themes about the teen experience.

PAUSE: First, let's discuss certain behaviours and emotions that are typical in the teenage years. Discuss the following questions with a small group.

1 What are some physical and emotional changes usually experienced in the teenage years?

2 Why do teenagers face additional expectations? Have you been expected to do anything differently now that you are a teen?

3 How has technology and social media has changed the experience of being a teen?

Kids these days

Although technology has developed in recent decades, teens have long experienced similar emotions and situations. As teens move out of childhood and towards adulthood, they start to develop their own ideas about the world and try to find their place in it. Teens search for identity and may challenge boundaries as they learn more about who they are and what is important to them. Of course, this process may be influenced by external influences, such as parents, friends, media and social expectations. However, despite the time period, there are many shared experiences felt by teens. Some of these ideas are featured in the following diagram.

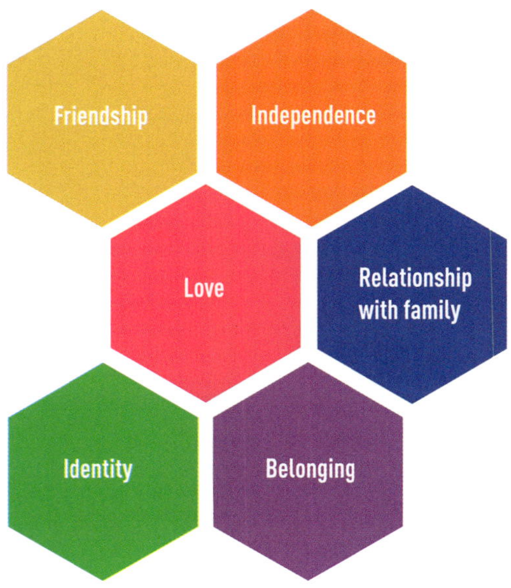

When it comes to reflecting the teen experience, some older texts have been transformed and recreated for a different context, purpose or audience to show how experiences of the teenage years have changed or remained the same.

It is called **intertextuality** when a text draws on another text or recreates an old one in a new context. As a reader or viewer, it is important to always think about why the text references another text and why it has been transformed. What does the composer of the new text want to show about the new context? What does the new text show us about our world?

One form of intertextuality is **appropriation.**

You are now going to examine some texts that have been **appropriated** for different contexts. Consider what the texts reflect about teens in each context.

> **VOCABULARY**
>
> **Context**
> Context means the setting of a text. Setting here means more than just location. This also includes the time period the text is set in and the social, historical or cultural influences this setting has on the meaning of the text.

> **VOCABULARY**
>
> **Intertextuality**
> Intertextuality is when a text draws on or refers to another text. References to another text can be obvious but they can also be made through other features such as characters or storylines.

> **VOCABULARY**
>
> **Appropriation**
> Appropriation occurs when an element of an original text (like the characters or plot) is used in a new text in a different context.

Twelfth Night (1601) and *She's the Man* (2006)

4.10.6 Understanding and responding to texts C

1 Research the plot of William Shakespeare's play *Twelfth Night* (written in the early 1600s). List some of the play's main events.

2 Find and watch the trailer for the film *She's the Man* (2006). List the events from the film that are similar to the plot of *Twelfth Night*.

3 How does the film reflect teens in this modern context? (Consider the way the characters act, talk and dress.)

The Karate Kid (1984 and 2010)

4.10.7 Understanding and responding to texts C

Research the plot of *The Karate Kid* (1984). From your research, what are some issues that teens face in this context?

Find and watch the 'Sand the Floor' scene from *The Karate Kid* (1984). Then find the 'Pick Up Your Jacket' scene from *The Karate Kid* (2010).

Complete the Venn diagram to compare what the texts reflect about teens.

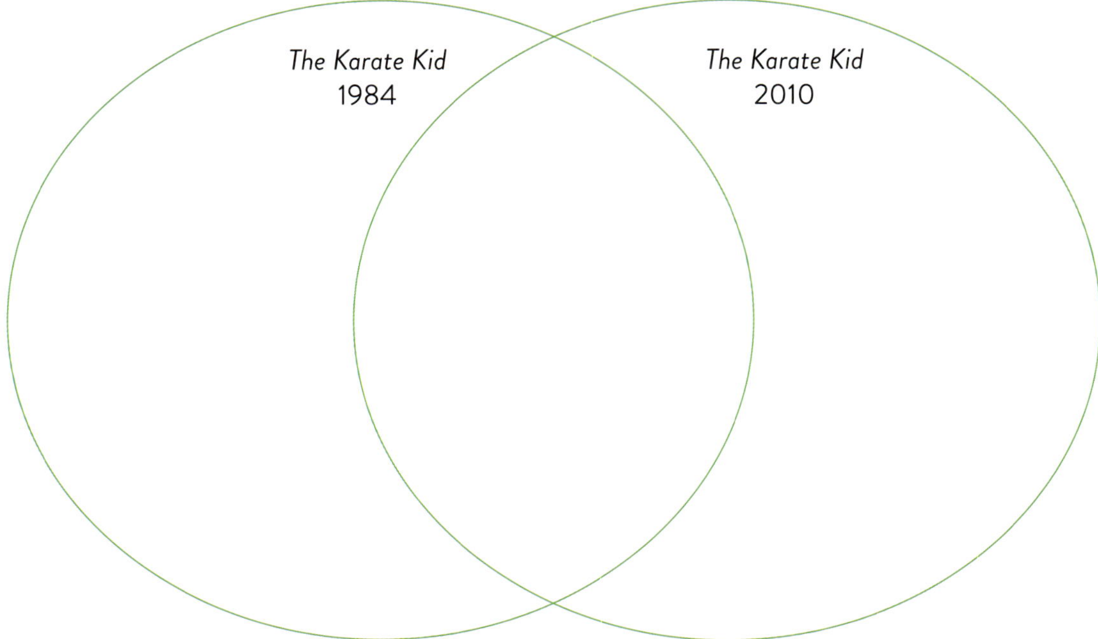

You have seen how texts about teens can be **appropriated** for different contexts. Remember, it is always important to think about why the text has been appropriated and what new ideas are generated from this transformation. You will now express your ideas about what viewers can learn from the appropriation of one of the texts above.

4.10.8 Expressing ideas and composing texts A

Explain how one textual appropriation (*She's the Man* [2006] or *The Karate Kid* [2010]) reflects teens in a modern context.

Use the scaffold below to compose your **analytical response**.

Structure of response	Language to use	Write your response
Topic sentence: Identify an idea about what an appropriated text reflects about teens.		
Explanation: Explain how this appropriated version captures the experience of teens in the modern world.	**Cause and effect:** *because, as a result of, consequently*	
Textual evidence: Discuss how the text has been appropriated from the original text.	**Comparative:** *similarly, also, alike, in the same way, contrastingly, on the other hand, however*	
Personal response: What does this appropriation tell you about the teen experience?	**Evaluative:** *effective, accurate/ inaccurate, appropriate/ inappropriate*	

4.10.9 Chapter reflection

1 What do you think are the most important experiences shared by teens? Identify two experiences shared by teens around the world and explain why these are important in this stage of life.

Teen experience	Why this is an important experience

2 Find a text that you have recently read or viewed and complete the following tasks.

a Give a summary of the plot and characters of this text.

b Explain what themes this text reflects about teens.

3 Choose a well-known fairy tale and consider how this could be appropriated for teens in our modern context. Write a summary of how you would appropriate the tale to reflect an issue that modern teens face.

4 Let's return to the unit inquiry question: ***How do the themes and language of film texts celebrate teens?*** How have your reading and viewing experiences in this chapter addressed the inquiry question?

Chapter 11

The Hunt for the Modern Teen

Chapter overview

In this chapter you will learn the language of film to be able to examine how themes are reflected in film texts. You will closely examine the film *Hunt for the Wilderpeople*, directed by Taika Waititi, and consider what it reflects about the modern teen experience.

Success criteria: In this chapter, I will be successful when I can ...

- identify language used in film to convey ideas
- describe themes about the teen experience reflected in *Hunt for the Wilderpeople*
- explain how film language is used to convey themes about the teen experience
- compose analytical responses to communicate my ideas
- share my personal views on the issues faced by modern teens.

Chapter inquiry questions

- What is the language of film?
- How are themes about teens shown through film language in *Hunt for the Wilderpeople*?

Key vocabulary

- Camera work
- Editing
- Mise-en-scène
- Dialogue
- Music
- Symbol
- Theme

What is the language of film?

Just like novels and poems, films tell a story, share emotion and communicate through language. Film uses some of the same elements as other stories – such as characters, plot and theme – but it also uses both sound and visual language.

4.11.1 Warm-up

Recipe for a great film

What is needed to make a great film? Think about your favourite films and what you like about them. What do you see on screen that makes them enjoyable? What about what you can hear as you watch them?

Imagine you are writing a recipe to make a great film. Write a list of ingredients below.

Extension activity

A method in a recipe explains how to use the ingredients to create the final product. Now that you have your list of ingredients, can you write the method for how to use these ingredients to make a great film? Consider the order you would use these ingredients in and how they would be used.

When you examine a film, it is important to remember that the director has made a lot of choices about the details included in the film. The purpose of a film is to have an impact on the viewer, and the film language helps to achieve this.

Visual language of a film

First, let's explore some of the ways that films use visual language to communicate ideas.

Camera work

The position and angle of a camera allows viewers to see the subject in different ways.

Match each of the camera angles or shots to their definition. Then research each of these angles or shots online to see what it looks like on screen.

Camera angle		Definition
High angle		The camera is positioned as the eyes of the subject, so the viewer can see a situation in the same way as the subject.
Low angle		Shows a subject in close detail, usually focused on a particular part or aspect of the subject.
Over the shoulder		The camera is raised above the subject and is tilted down to make the subject appear small.
Point of view		Shows the subject from the waist up, makes the viewer feel involved in the scene.
Close up shot		The camera is positioned behind the subject as they face another person.
Medium shot		Shows a large section of a location or setting to show the viewer where the scene takes place.
Long shot		The camera is positioned near the ground and points up at the subject, making them appear bigger.
Extreme wide shot		Shows the full body of the subject and their surroundings.

Editing

A film is shot in different sections. These sections of film are then edited together to make a continuous film and have a desired impact on the viewer.

Research each of the following types of transitions, which are used in editing to move between scenes. Write your own definition and what impact you think this type of editing transition would have on the viewer.

Editing transition	Definition	What impact would this have on the viewer?
Cut		
Fade		
Montage		

Watch a scene from your favourite animated film. Identify one type of editing transition used in the film and explain the impact this has on the viewer.

____

____

Mise-en-scène

Mise-en-scène refers to the arrangement of everything that is captured by the camera, such as costumes, lighting, set and props, locations and special effects. Putting all these pieces together creates a believable scene and will help to tell the story on screen.

Examine this still from a film scene. Explain how the elements listed contribute to the emotion of this scene.

- Location
- Lighting
- Props
- Costume

____

____

____

Sound language of a film

Of course, the main sound heard in film is the **dialogue** spoken between characters. But let's explore some of the other ways that films use sound to communicate ideas.

Music

Music might be heard within the scene of a film or added later during the editing process. Music helps to convey emotion in a scene, impacting viewers to feel the same, and it can leave a lasting, memorable impression.

In a small group, research the most memorable music moments in film. Listen to some of the songs and if you don't know the movie, discuss what emotion you think the music raises for the viewer.

Sound effects

Sound effects are added during the editing process. Advances in technology have meant that these sound effects are more realistic and make viewers feel more involved in the action of the scene.

Choose one of the following general scenes and discuss with a group what sound effects could be added to make the scene realistic: car chase, sitting in a classroom, walking on the beach or a wedding.

Silence

Sometimes silence is just as powerful as sound! A lack of sound can emphasise emotion for the viewer or add to the atmosphere of the scene.

In a group, discuss possible scenes where silence or a lack of sound would be powerful. Now that you have been introduced to the language of film, apply your knowledge to viewing a film text.

4.11.2 Viewing texts

Find and watch the 'Stolen Generations' scene from the film *Rabbit Proof Fence*, directed by Phillip Noyce. In this scene, three Aboriginal children are forcibly taken from their mother and grandmother. As you watch the scene, consider how film language adds to the emotional impact of this scene.

1 What emotional impact does this scene have on viewers?

____

____

2 Identify and explain how two aspects of film language (visual or sound) are used to create this emotional impact.

Film language	Example from the scene	Impact on the viewer

How are themes about teens shown through film language in *Hunt for the Wilderpeople*?

Hunt for the Wilderpeople (2016) is a film directed by Taika Waititi and set in New Zealand. The film tells the story of rebellious teen Ricky Baker who has been rejected from several foster homes. He finally feels accepted in the home of Bella and Hec. However, after Bella dies unexpectedly and child services declare that they will move Ricky to another home, he runs away into the wilderness. Hec follows Ricky and after they become stranded in the bush, they become the subject of a national manhunt as police mistakenly think Hec has kidnapped Ricky. Although Hec is bad-tempered, he and Ricky form an unlikely bond to survive in the bush.

PAUSE: The film has been adapted from the novel *Wild Pork and Watercress* by Barry Crump. This is a form of **intertextuality** (go back to Chapter 10 if you need a reminder about this term).

Research the plot for the novel and compare with the plot of the film. What is the same and what is different? What do the differences tell you about the film's purpose?

The film is structured in chapters. There are 10 chapters plus an epilogue, which provides a conclusion to the story. The use of chapters in the film, like a book, is important because Ricky loves the written word, often sharing his poems and reading stories aloud to Hec. On the other hand, Hec cannot read but learns to appreciate stories through Ricky's influence. The chapter structure also allows readers to see the growth in Ricky's character and his relationship with Hec. The chapter titles also give you a hint about the main idea in each part of the film.

4.11.3 Viewing texts

As you watch the film, record what happens in each chapter and what you learn about the main characters.

Chapter	What are the main events of this chapter?	What do you learn about Ricky and/or Hec?
A Real Bad Egg		
Another Door		
Goodbye, Ricky Baker		
Broken Foot Camp		
Famous		
Close to the Sky		
A Normal Life		
The Knack		
Turn of the Tide		
War		
Epilogue		

The film reflects several ideas about the modern teen experience. In this section you will closely explore each idea and examine key scenes from the film to determine what themes are reflected about these ideas.

Belonging

A key idea reflected in the film is belonging, as Ricky struggles to find a family that accepts him. Viewers see that for most of his early life, Ricky has been rejected from foster homes and as a result has developed a limited sense of belonging.

View the opening scene 'A Real Bad Egg', from 2:00 to 4:50, and consider how Ricky's background has been introduced to viewers.

4.11.4 Viewing texts

1 What impression do you think viewers have of Ricky from this opening?

2 What does the **montage** reveal about how Ricky has responded to his lack of belonging?

3 Paula, from child services, calls Ricky 'a real bad egg' and tells him that 'there's no one else who wants you'. How do you think this might affect Ricky's sense of identity?

Although Ricky pretends to escape every night from his new home with Bella and Hec, he always returns as he enjoys his time at the farm and starts to feel a sense of belonging.

View the 'First Birthday' scene from 14:10 to 15:20.

4.11.5 Viewing texts

1 What do you think this scene shows about Ricky's sense of belonging? Support your answer with one line of **dialogue** from the scene.

2 The very next scene after this is Bella's unexpected death. Why do you think these two scenes have been **edited** next to each other? What does this suggest about what Ricky may be thinking or feeling?

3 **A symbol of Ricky's sense of belonging is the hot water bottle. What comes to mind when you think of a hot water bottle? What do you think this shows about Ricky's sense of belonging?**

____

____

View both the opening chapter 'A Real Bad Egg' and the Epilogue at the end of the film. Look for the hot water bottle and then complete the activity below.

VOCABULARY

Symbol
Remember, a symbol is used to represent or show a larger idea, action or feeling. A symbol may be an object, character or place.

4.11.6 Viewing texts

Fill the empty hot water bottle with ideas about what it could symbolise about Ricky's sense of belonging.

As the film progresses and Ricky and Hec are left to survive in the wilderness together, they learn more about each other and develop a close relationship. Although they aren't family in a traditional sense, they develop their own sense of family. Loyalty becomes an important part of their relationship.

View the scene 'Zag's Death' from 1:03:00 to 1:07:50. Dogs are often considered 'man's best friend' and are known to be loyal. In this scene, it is not only the dogs that show loyalty to Hec. Examine how film language is used to reflect the change in Ricky and Hec's relationship.

 4.11.7 Understanding and responding to texts B 

1 At the beginning of this scene Ricky says, 'I'm better at being a gangster'. What does Ricky's longing to be a gangster tell you about his sense of belonging?

____

____

2 How does Ricky display loyalty to Hec in this scene?

____

____

3 Describe the **music** when Hec releases Bella's ashes into the waterfall. Why has this music been used?

____

____

4 What do you think this scene suggests about family? Explain your response with reference to a specific part of this scene.

____

____

Now that you have explored some key scenes that reflect the idea of belonging, it's time to draw out some of the **themes** reflected in the text about belonging as part of the teen experience.

Hint: Go back to Chapter 10 if you need a reminder about themes.

Complete the 'See, Think, Me, We' activity below to organise your thinking.

4.11.8 Understanding and responding to texts B 

SEE: Look closely at the film. What do you see about belonging?	THINK: What message about belonging do you think the director wants to share for teenagers?
ME: What is your personal response to this? How can you connect this to your life and experience as a teen?	**WE: How could this film be connected to the experience of other teens? Why does this text have value?**

Now, you will be guided in how to compose an analytical response that communicates how the theme of belonging is reflected in the text.

4.11.9 Expressing ideas and composing texts A

Complete the cloze passage below, using the responses you have written in the activities above.

The film *Hunt for the Wilderpeople* shows that for teens belonging is ______________________________

____.

Belonging is an important concept for the teen protagonist of the film because ____________________

____.

In the beginning of the film, Ricky is shown as ______________________________________.

This is reflected in the opening montage through images of ______________________________

____.

Ricky's identity is also impacted by ____.

However, as the film progresses and Ricky spends more time with Hec, he learns that belonging

to family is ____.

This idea is reflected through the film language of __________________________________.

Another scene that shows Ricky's new sense of belonging is when ____________________

____________________.

The use of ____________________ in this scene shows that

____________________.

By the end of the film, Ricky understands that belonging is ____________________

____________________.

Therefore, the film shows that for teens ____________________

____

____________________.

Expressing feelings and dealing with loss

Another key idea reflected in the film is how teens and adults express their feelings and deal with loss. While Ricky is initially shown to have resorted to disobedience following his troubled family life, he is the one who teaches Hec how to express emotions positively and deal with loss. You know that teenagers experience a variety of emotions, and one of the most important lessons in life is how to positively move through these emotions.

Ricky uses haiku poetry to express his emotions and deal with his feelings. He tells Bella that a counsellor once gave him this strategy.

PAUSE: Do you know what a haiku is? If you know, teach your peers about the rules of a haiku, otherwise research it online and read some examples.

4.11.10 Viewing texts

View the following scenes from the beginning, middle and end of the film. Read the haikus that Ricky creates at each of these stages of his development plus Hec's haiku at the end of the film.

Maggots 10:30–12:30	Running 1:13:00–1:14:00	Hec's Haiku 1:27:00–1:30:35
There's heaps of maggots – *Maggots wriggling in that sheep* *Like moving rice. Yuck.*	*Trees, birds, rivers, sky.* *Running with my Uncle Hec.* *Living forever.*	*Me and this fat kid* *We ran, we ate and read books* *And it was the best.*

1 Compare Ricky's two haikus, 'Maggots' and 'Running'. What do these haikus tell you about how he has changed and developed over the course of the film?

___

___

2 Throughout the film, Hec struggles to express his emotions and instead often resorts to silence or anger. What does Hec's haiku at the end of the film tell you about what he has learned from Ricky?

___

___

Both Ricky and Hec have experienced loss and must find ways to deal with loss. Ricky has lost his birth mother and biological family and Hec loses Bella. Hec tries to run away from his grief, thinking that if he escapes into the wilderness he can run away from his loss. However, this is where his healing occurs. Hec's character is important for teens because he is an example of an adult who didn't learn to express his emotions as a teen. But we see that it's never too late and Hec learns to express his emotions more positively by the end of the film.

4.11.11 Understanding and responding to texts B

View the following scenes that show the different ways that Ricky and Hec react to loss. For each scene, write a description of how each character responds to loss and how the film language shows this to the audience.

	Hec **Bella's Funeral: 17:30–23:10**	**Ricky** **Psycho Sam: 1:11:00–1:15:40**
How does the character respond to loss?		
How does film language show this character's response to the audience?		

When Hec breaks his foot, he is literally forced to sit and reflect on his feelings. This is a turning point for his character as he learns from Ricky about how to deal with emotions. Ricky learns about **resilience** from Hec as he teaches Ricky to survive in the wilderness and rely on his own instincts.

> **VOCABULARY**
>
> **Resilience**
> *noun* the ability to cope with difficulties and move forward after challenges.

View the 'Broken Foot' scene from 28:00 to 35:00.

4.11.12 Understanding and responding to texts B

Explain what this scene shows about the theme of expressing emotions and dealing with grief. Support your response with examples of TWO of the following features of film language:

Camera work	Mise-en-scène	Editing	Dialogue	Music

The choice of setting for this film is also symbolic of the importance of resilience for teens. When he is first lost in the bush, Ricky finds it difficult to survive (see the montage from 25:00 to 27:00). Slowly his skills improve. He learns about 'The Knack' from Hec (view the film at 31:20 to see an explanation of this) and learns to trust himself.

View the **montage** of Ricky and Hec from 41:00 to 44:00 in the middle of the film.

4.11.13 Viewing texts

How do the visual and sound languages of film in this montage show that Ricky and Hec are growing stronger in their ability to survive together? Discuss specific aspects of film language to support your response.

The end of the film celebrates the resilience of both characters, who have survived and grown stronger as a result of their ability to accept their losses and rely on their own instincts.

View the Epilogue from 1:27:00 to the end of the film and complete the reflection opposite.

4.11.14 Viewing reflection

What is your response to the end of the film? Do you feel satisfied with this ending? What are the final takeaways about the characters?

Let's bring together your thoughts about what themes the film shows about dealing with loss and emotions as a crucial part of the teen experience.

4.11.15 Expressing ideas and composing texts A

Compose an analytical paragraph that explains how one theme about loss, emotions or resilience for teens is shown through film language. Refer to two scenes from the film in your response. Use the scaffold below to compose your **analytical response**.

Structure of response	Write your response
Topic sentence: Identify a theme that the film shows about loss, emotions or resilience for teens.	
Explanation: Explain why this is an important theme for teens and why the film has value in sharing this theme.	
Textual evidence: Discuss how film language has been used in two scenes to show this theme. Provide explanations of how these scenes show the theme.	
Personal response: Why do you think teens might connect with this theme in the film? What do you think others could learn from viewing this theme?	

4.11.16 Chapter reflection

1 What have you learned about the language of film?

2 What did you most enjoy about the film *Hunt for the Wilderpeople?*

3 What do you think the film shows about life for modern teens?

4 Let's return to the unit inquiry question: ***How do the themes and language of film texts celebrate teens?*** How have your reading and viewing experiences in this chapter addressed the inquiry question?

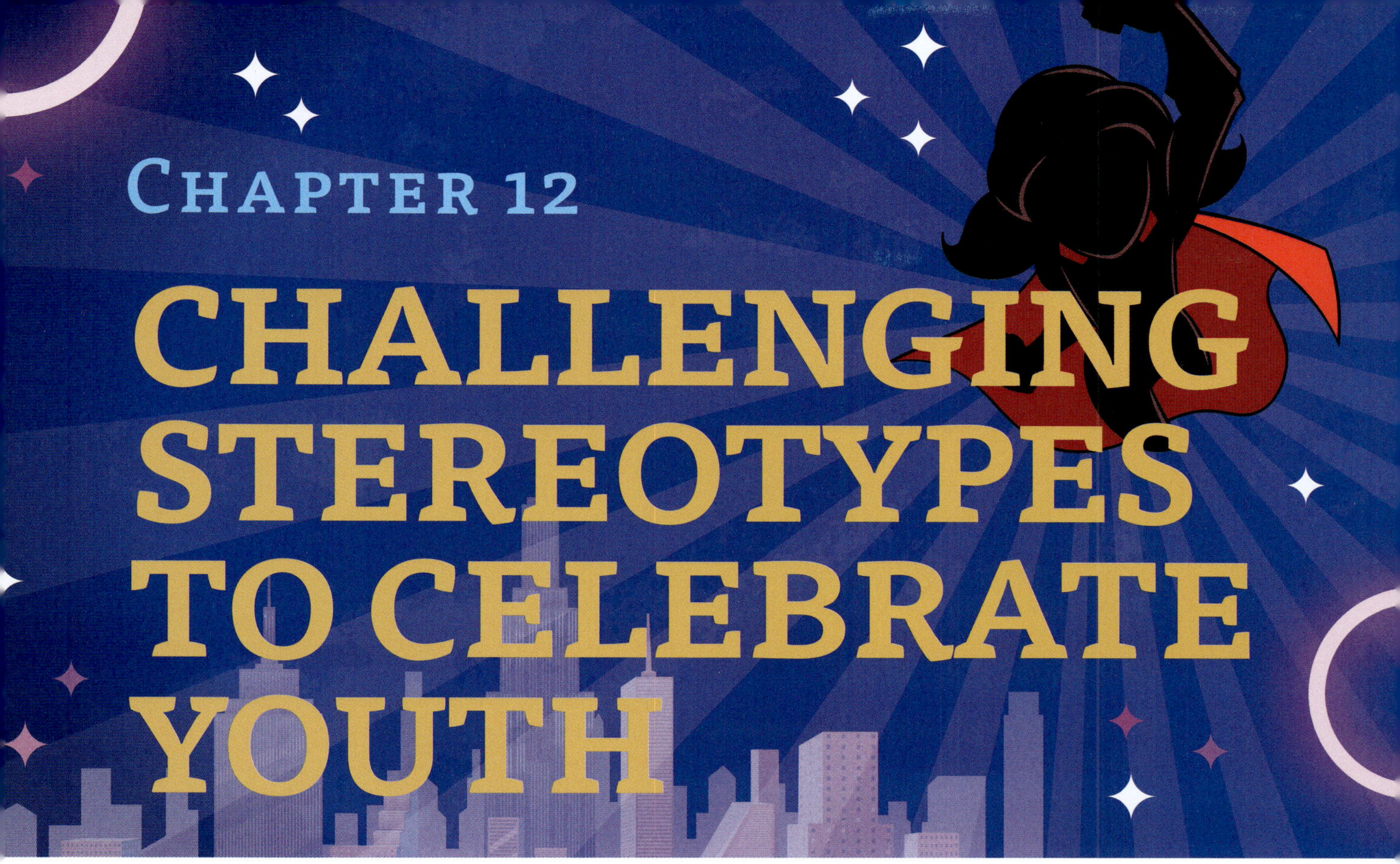

Chapter 12

CHALLENGING STEREOTYPES TO CELEBRATE YOUTH

Chapter overview

In this chapter you will learn how texts can challenge stereotypes of teens. You will also analyse how film texts celebrate youth and teens in our world. You will communicate your ideas in extended analytical responses, drawing on the texts examined and your learning from this unit to develop your ideas logically. In order to successfully complete this chapter you will need to watch segments of the following films:

Brave (2012): 'Archery' scene

Big Hero 6 (2014): 'Hiro's Idea' scene

Inside Out (2015): 'First Day at School' scene

The Promise (2020), directed and produced by Chi Thai

Loop Pixar (2020), SparkShorts trailer of the film

Success criteria: In this chapter, I will be successful when I can ...

- identify stereotypes of teens in texts
- describe how stereotypes have been challenged in texts to celebrate teens
- explain how film language is used to challenge ideas about teens
- support personal responses with textual evidence
- compose analytical responses to communicate my ideas.

Chapter inquiry questions

- What stereotypes of teens are challenged by film texts?
- What do film texts celebrate about teens?
- How can I communicate my ideas about how texts celebrate teens in extended analytical responses?

Key vocabulary

- Stereotypes
- Challenge
- Celebrate
- Literary value
- Analytical response

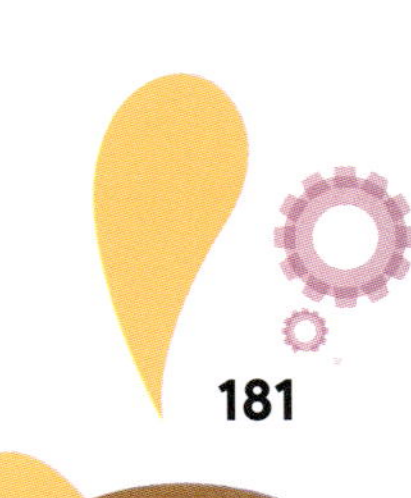

What stereotypes of teens are challenged by film texts?

There may have been times when you have felt frustrated that an adult has assumed you will act a certain way because you are a teenager. This is known as a **stereotype.**

VOCABULARY

Stereotype
A stereotype is a simplistic view that people have of a particular thing or person. Stereotypes assume that all people in a group have similar characteristics.

4.12.1 Warm-up

Where do you stand?

Read the statements below about teenagers. Tick whether you agree or disagree with each statement.

Statement	Agree	Disagree
It is easy to be a teenager.		
Teens are too young to understand serious topics.		
All teenagers make decisions without thinking of consequences.		
Teens these days wouldn't last a day without their phone.		
Teenagers are emotional.		

Choose ONE statement and list three reasons to support why you agree or disagree.

- ______________________________
- ______________________________
- ______________________________

Come together in a small group and discuss your opinions on these statements.

One of the great things about having texts in our world, like novels and films, is that they can help to challenge stereotypes and show different experiences for people.

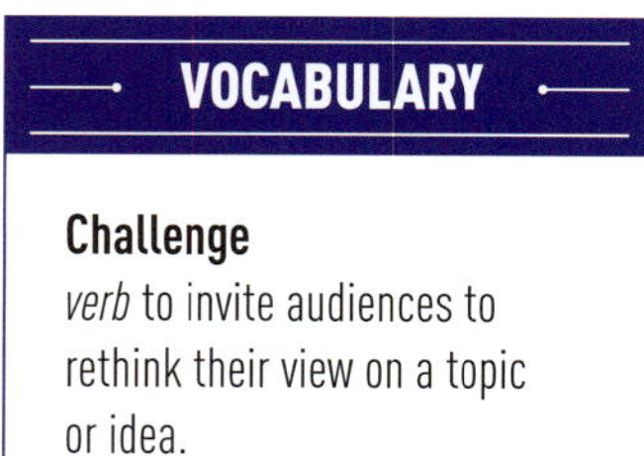

PAUSE: Before you examine how films challenge stereotypes of teens, you need to consider what stereotypes of teens exist in our world.

In a small group, make a list of at least ten stereotypes that exist about teens. You were presented with some in the warm-up activity, so use this as a starting point for your discussion.

Now you will view scenes from some films that challenge stereotypes of teens.

4.12.2 Viewing texts

Research the plot of each of the films listed below. Then view the film scenes and consider what stereotypes of teens are challenged.

Brave (2012): 'Archery' scene
Big Hero 6 (2014): 'Hiro's Idea' scene
Inside Out (2015): 'First Day at School' scene

Identify two stereotypes of teens that are challenged in these film scenes and explain what you see in the films to support each idea.

	Stereotype 1: ______________	**Stereotype 2:** ______________
What makes you say this stereotype is challenged?		
What do you see in the film scenes that makes you say this stereotype is challenged?		

4.12.3 Expressing ideas and composing texts A

Personal response

What other stereotypes of teens would you like to see challenged in more film texts? Why is this important to you?

____

____

____

____

____

What do film texts celebrate about teens?

Now that you have examined how film texts challenge stereotypes of teens, let's look at how films celebrate teens. In this context, celebrate means to praise or appreciate the qualities of teens as an important part of our world. While teens may sometimes have a bad reputation, teens have wonderful qualities such as optimism for the future, energy and motivation, a sense of humour, creativity and a willingness to try new things .

You will now be guided in analysing some short films that celebrate other qualities of teens. You will also consider the **literary value** of these films. You will also be required to discuss how film language is used to share ideas about teens. Here is a reminder of some features of film language. Go back to Chapter 11 if you need a reminder of these features.

VOCABULARY

Literary value
Remember, literary value means that a text reflects important ideas for our society. It also means that the text and its ideas are relevant for people from different contexts and may encourage readers to reflect on their own life and values.

Camera angles and shots	Editing	Mise-en-scène	Dialogue	Music	Sound effects	Silence

▶▶ Find and watch the short film *The Promise*, directed and produced by Chi Thai (running time: 6:42).

4.11.4 Understanding and responding to texts C

1 Describe the world before and after the acorn is planted. How does the film language show these two different worlds?

2 A **voiceover** is used throughout the film, in which the narrator tells the story of how she stole the bag and made a promise to plant the acorns. What do you learn about the character from this voiceover?

3 What does this film celebrate about the importance of teens for the future of our planet?

Find and watch the trailer on a short film *Loop* by Pixar SparkShorts.

4.11.5 Understanding and responding to texts C

1 What do you think viewers could learn from each character about understanding others and showing compassion? Explain your thoughts.

Character	Renee	Marcus
What could viewers learn about understanding others and showing compassion from this character?		
Why do you think this is important in our world today?		

2 Renee is autistic, and she is non-verbal, which means she doesn't speak. However, she has a powerful voice in this film. Explain how she is celebrated and appreciated in this film.

3 Choose one film language feature that you think was used well in this film. Explain your reasoning with examples from the film.

4.12.6 Viewing reflection

What other films or television shows have you viewed that you think show an appreciation of teens? Discuss how this film celebrates teens and why others should view it.

How can I communicate my ideas about how texts celebrate teens in extended analytical responses?

You have explored how texts celebrate the important role teens play in our society. You will now learn how to communicate your ideas in an extended analytical response.

You learned in Chapter 10 that an **analytical response** shares a perspective by presenting logically sequenced ideas. In this type of response, you will look closely at a text to support your ideas and examine the way it uses language to communicate ideas. An extended analytical response is structured with an **introduction**, a **body** and a **conclusion**. Each of these sections has an important role.

Introduction

- States the main idea or argument presented in the response.
- Introduces the text/s that will be referenced to support ideas.
- Outlines the supporting ideas that will be discussed in each paragraph to develop the main idea of the response.

Body

- Paragraphs are used to discuss different ideas, all connected to the main idea of the response.
- Ideas are explained in each paragraph with reference to examples and language of the text/s.
- Personal interpretation of the text is provided – i.e why the text is important in relation to the main idea of the paragraph.

Conclusion

- Reinforces the main idea of the response.
- Provides an overall comment on why this idea is important or what audiences can learn from reading/viewing the text examined.

Read the introduction paragraph about how the Disney film *Moana* celebrates teens. Examine how the paragraph has been structured and written.

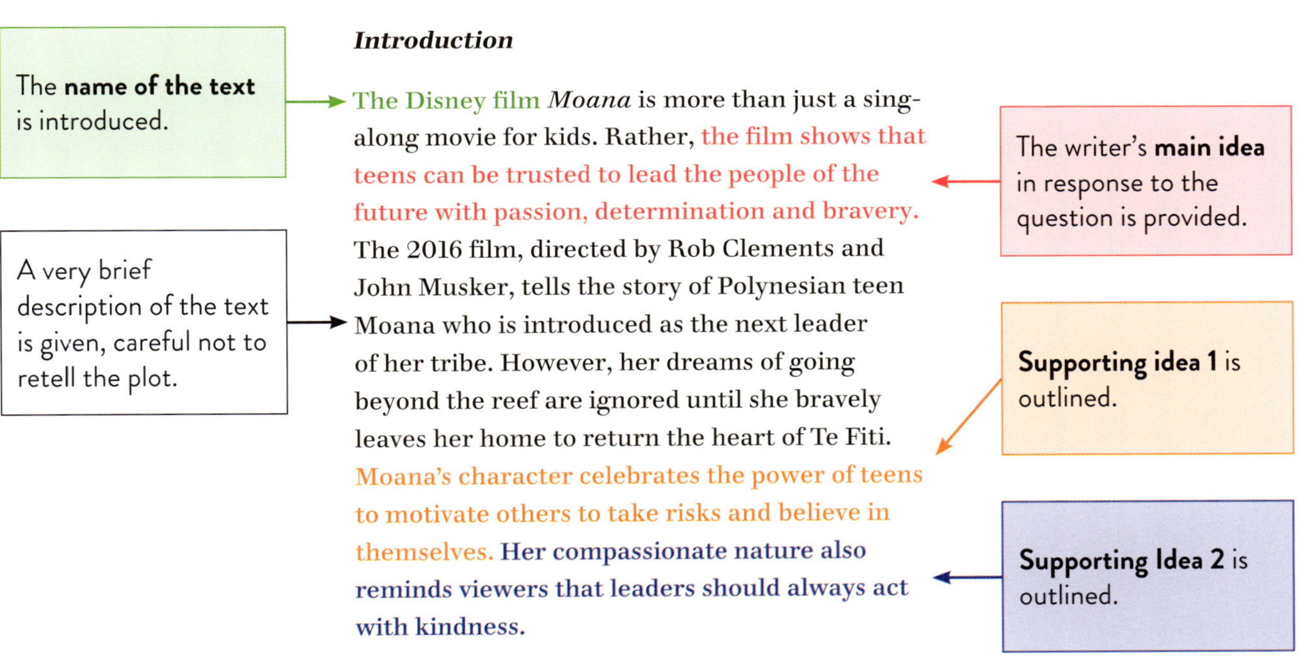

How does the film *Moana* successfully celebrate teens?

Introduction

The Disney film *Moana* is more than just a sing-along movie for kids. Rather, the film shows that teens can be trusted to lead the people of the future with passion, determination and bravery. The 2016 film, directed by Rob Clements and John Musker, tells the story of Polynesian teen Moana who is introduced as the next leader of her tribe. However, her dreams of going beyond the reef are ignored until she bravely leaves her home to return the heart of Te Fiti. Moana's character celebrates the power of teens to motivate others to take risks and believe in themselves. Her compassionate nature also reminds viewers that leaders should always act with kindness.

4.12.7 Expressing ideas and composing texts B

Create an introduction paragraph for your own analytical response that explains how one film text you have examined in this unit celebrates teens.

Use the introduction sample and the planning table below to guide you.

Chosen film text: Name, date and director details	
Main idea: What does this film celebrate about teens?	
Supporting ideas: What ideas will be discussed to support this main idea about how teens are celebrated?	

Write your introduction here.

Now read the sample body paragraph that follows this introduction. Look closely at how ideas are developed with reference to the film and its language.

Body paragraph

The **topic sentence** outlines the idea of the paragraph. Notice how this matches what was outlined in the introduction.

Connection made between the text and the experience of teens.

This section explains how film language (bolded) is used to show ideas about Moana's bravery and willingness to take risks.

Moana's character celebrates the power of teens to motivate others to take risks and believe in themselves. Teens can sometimes struggle to have confidence in their own abilities and often life presents challenges that can make teens feel vulnerable. The opening of the film establishes that Moana lives an easy life in her village and will one day be the next leader of her people. The **mise-en-scène** of bright colours, the beautiful beach and her people sharing and caring for one other show that she could live happily on the island. However, soon the coconuts start to rot on the island and the number of fish caught decreases. She tries to solve the problem by suggesting to her father that she leave the island and sail beyond the reef to find more fish, but he disapproves. Moana is encouraged by Gramma Tala, who asks 'Do you really think our ancestors stayed within the reef?' When Moana sneaks into the water, she is overpowered by the ocean. The colours change in this scene from bright colours to dark, terrifying colours creating a change in mood from cheerful to frightening as Moana starts to face difficulty. **Low angle camera angles** are used to show the huge size of the waves compared to Moana's little boat, showing the difficulty she is facing. Even though she returns to the island after this event, Moana later goes back out into the ocean and sails beyond the reef. These examples show that Moana is willing to take risks for her people, unlike the adults on the island who are unwilling to try. She also shows resilience by going back out to the reef. In this way, the film celebrates the bravery of teens and shows that the world is in safe hands with the next generation of leaders.

Return to the idea of the paragraph, providing a **personal interpretation** about the importance and value of the text.

4.12.8 Expressing ideas and composing texts B

Write a body paragraph that follows the introduction you wrote in Activity 4.12.7. Refer to the way film language is used in the chosen film to support your discussion.

Use the body paragraph sample and the planning table below to guide you.

Topic sentence: What idea will this paragraph discuss that supports the main idea of the response?	
Text analysis: How does the text support this idea? What film language will you discuss?	
Personal interpretation: What point will you make about why this idea is important? What can others learn from this?	

Write your body paragraph here.

4.12.9 Chapter reflection

1 Complete the '4 Cs' chart below to show what you have learned about the way teens are reflected and celebrated in film texts.

Connections: What connections can you make between the teen characters you have examined and your life?	**Challenge**: What text do you think was the most effective at challenging stereotypes of teens?
Concepts: What concepts or themes reflected in the texts about teens in this unit are the most valuable?	**Changes**: What changes in the way you write have come about for you following your learning in this unit?

2 What have you learned about your strengths in writing analytical responses?

______

______

______

3 In what areas of writing an analytical response do you require further support?

______

______

______

4 Let's return to the unit inquiry question: ***How do the themes and language of film texts celebrate teens?*** How have your reading and viewing experiences in this unit addressed the inquiry question?

______

______

______

______

Unit 4: Summative assessment

The summative assessment options below provide opportunities to demonstrate your achievement of the following outcomes and focus areas:

Outcome	EN4-RVL-01 Reading, viewing and listening to texts	EN4-URB-01 Understanding and responding to texts B	EN4-URC-01 Understanding and responding to texts C	EN4-ECA-01 Expressing ideas and composing texts A	EN4-ECB-01 Expressing ideas and composing texts B
Focus Area	Reading, viewing and listening for meaning	Theme	Intertextuality Literary value	Text features: informative and analytical	Planning, monitoring and revising

Option 1:

Teens have a lot to teach adults.

Write an extended analytical response that explains how one teen character of a film text examined in this unit reflects important themes and lessons. Discuss how film language is used to celebrate this teen character.

Ensure your response ...

- outlines a main idea in response to the question
- develops ideas in a logically structured **analytical response**
- explains how **film language** is used to reflect important **themes** about being a teen
- provides a judgement on the **literary value** of the character and film text
- if relevant, discusses the way the text has drawn on other texts in a different context (**intertextuality**) to reflect the teen experience.

Option 2:

A great film can challenge viewers to think differently.

How has one film text examined in this unit challenged viewers to think differently about teens? Write an analytical response that discusses the film language used in this film to have this impact on the audience.

Ensure your response ...

- outlines a main idea in response to the question
- develops ideas in a logically structured **analytical response**
- explains how **film language** is used to reflect important **themes** about being a teen
- provides a judgement on the **literary value** of the character and film text
- if relevant, discusses the way the text has drawn on other texts in a different context (**intertextuality**) to reflect the teen experience.

Option 3:

Do you agree that *The Hunt for the Wilderpeople* successfully celebrates the importance of teens in our world?

Write an analytical response to the question above that explains how the film reflects important themes about the teen experience. Discuss how film language is used in at least two key scenes from the film.

Ensure your response ...

- outlines a main idea in response to the question
- develops ideas in a logically structured **analytical response**
- explains how **film language** is used to reflect important **themes** about being a teen
- provides a judgement on the **literary value** of the character and film text.

Assessment as Learning: Self-Assessment

Does my response:

- ☐ present an overall idea about the way the film reflects the teen experience?
- ☐ explain how film language of the chosen film is used to support ideas?
- ☐ develop ideas logically and use appropriate structure and language?
- ☐ provide a judgement on the literary value of the text?

What are two strengths of my response?

____

____

____

What area/s of my response do I need to refine further?

____

____

____

ACKNOWLEDGEMENTS

Insight Publications thanks the author, Emily Beach, for all her work on *English for NSW, Year 7, Stage 4*. Insight Publications is also grateful to the following individuals and organisations for permission to reproduce copyright material.

Texts: NESA website: English K-10 Syllabus © NSW Education Standards Authority for and on behalf of the Crown in right of the State of New South Wales, 2012; Extract reprinted with permission from 'True Spirit' by Jessica Watson, Hachette Australia Books 2022; Extract reprinted with permission from 'Songs of a War Boy' by Deng Thiak Adut, Hachette Australia, 2019.M13; 'The Lessons Stan Grant hopes to pass onto his sons' by Stan Grant, The Sydney Morning Herald; Extract reprinted from Dylan Alcott 2022 Australian of the Year speech; 'How social media affects children at different ages – and how to protect them' by Daria Kuss, Nottingham Trent University, *The Conversation;* Extract: 'I call Australia home now, but I feel lucky that I've held onto my culture' by Shayan, ABC Heywire; Extract: 'Forever Fixing' by El Gibbs, Black Inc; 'Life of Pi's acidic island a warning for our warming world' by Thomas Faunce, Australian National University, *The Conversation*; 'The world's oldest story? Astronomers say global myths about 'seven sisters' stars may reach back 100,000 years' by Ray Norris, Western Sydney University, *The Conversation*; 'From Little Things, Big Things Grow'. Words and music by Kev Carmody and Paul Kelly © Copyright Sony/ATV Music Publishing Australia Pty Ltd and Song Cycles Pty Ltd administered by Kobalt Music Publishing Australia Pty Ltd Print rights for Kobalt Music Publishing Australia Pty Ltd administered in Australia and New Zealand by Hal Leonard Australia Pty Ltd ABN 13 085 333 713 www.halleonard.com.au Used By Permission. All Rights Reserved. Unauthorised Reproduction is Illegal; 'Legal consequences of online behaviour' eSafety Commissioner, Australian Government; 'Encanto, TikTok and the art of social storytelling: why music is not just for listening anymore' by Kai Riemer and Sandra Peter, University of Sydney, *The Conversation*; Text © 2011 Patrick Ness, from an original idea by Siobhan Dowd from A MONSTER CALLS, written by Patrick Ness, reproduced by permission of Walker Books Ltd, London, SE11 5HJ www.walker.co.uk 2; Text from Padraig ÔTuama; 'Mulga Bill's Bicycle' by Banjo Paterson, Sydney Mail; 'Maths Class' by Kirli Saunders, Magabala Books; 'Limelight' by Solli Raphael, Penguin Books Australia; 'Play on' by Omar Musa, Curtis Brown Australia; Extract: 'Boy Overboard: the Play' by Patricia Cornelius, Currency Press Pty Ltd, Sydney Australia, www.currency.com.au; Extract: 'Romeo and Juliet' – prologue by William Shakespeare; Extract: 'Two Weeks with the Queen: The Play' adapted by Mary Morris, Currency Press Pty Ltd, Sydney Australia, www.currency.com.au; Extract: 'A Ghost in my Suitcase' adapted by Vanessa Bates, Currency Press Pty Ltd, Sydney Australia, www.currency.com.au; Extracts from 'Sunshine Super Girl' by Andrea James © Andrea James, 2021, reproduced by permission from Currency Press Pty Ltd, Sydney Australia, www.currency.com.au; Extract: The Little Wave by Pip Harry, University of Queensland Press; Extract: 'Laurinda' by Alice Pung, Black Inc. 2014; Extract: 'Tomorrow when the War Began' by John Marsden, Pan Macmillan Australia; Extract: 'The Forest' by Anna Jacobson, Walker Books; '?' by Oodgeroo Noonuccal, John Wiley & Sons. Inc; Extract: 'How to Bee' by Bren MacDibble, Allen & Unwin; Extracts: 'Blueback' by Tim Winton, Penguin Books Australia; Extracts: 'Black Cockatoo' by Carl Merrison and Hakea Hustler, Magabala Books; Extract: 'August & Jones' by Pip Harry, Hachette Australia Books; Extract: 'Mikki and Me and the Out of Tune Tree' by Marion Roberts, Allen & Unwin; Haikus from 'Hunt for the Wilderpeople'.

Images: Cover image reproduced with permission from *Songs of a War Boy* By Deng Thiak Adut, Hachette Australia, 2019; Cover image *Happy (and other ridiculous aspirations)* by Turia Pitt, Penguin Books Australia; Stan Grant with his father, Stan Grant; Cover image 'Black Cockatoo' by Carl Merrison and Hakea Hustler, Magabala Books; The following images from Alamy: Jessica Watson; Cover: 'Spirited Away'; Cover: 'A Monster Calls'; Cover: 'Big Hero 6'; 'Red Dog' movie poster; 'Back to the outback' movie poster; 'Rabbit proof fence' movie poster; Movie Still from 'Hunt for the Wilderpeople'; 'Big hero 6' characters; 'Moana' posters; Additional images from Shutterstock and Studio Number One.

Notes

